Dark Fantasy Tarot

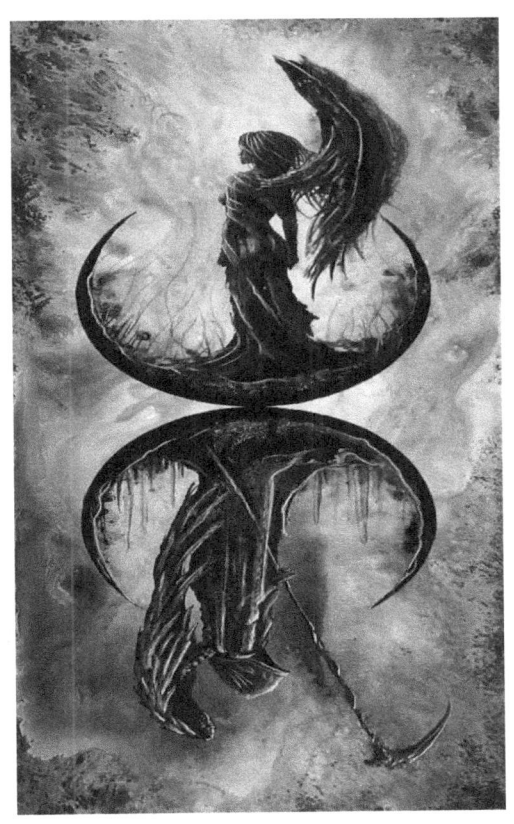

J Edward Neill

All Art by J Edward Neill

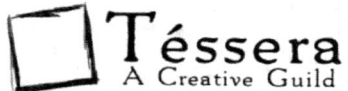

Copyright © 2024 J Edward Neill

All rights reserved

ISBN: 979-8338138113

Welcome to Dark Fantasy Tarot.

Over the last several years, I've created many tarot and oracle decks. All of them have arrived from a deep place within me, a glowing source of spiritual and artistic joy which I desperately need to express.

But this deck...this of *all* decks, was the most engrossing for me. I painted seventy-eight original canvasses, each one a labor of love. And for the first time, I wrote the guidebook without any co-authoring. My muse was singular, and my focus untouched by any other.

In my heart, I hope Dark Fantasy Tarot will be unlike all the other decks you may have befriended. I hope the art will reach out to your intuition, and I hope the very personal way I've crafted the card meanings will appeal to the truest version of yourself.

...the real you.
...the part beneath your everyday masks.

It's true – my expression of tarot art is perhaps darker than others. This is no accident. If my imagery seems rather shadowy, it's because I don't like pulling punches. You don't need a deck to playfully bump your ego with downy pillows. Soft landings might soothe you, but true shadow work means prying into places lying well out of the sunlight. Tough love is what they call it. If everything were rainbows and lollipops, I expect none of us would even need to try our hands at tarot.

Artistically, Dark Fantasy Tarot contains art spanning two years of work. The very first artwork completed (Temperance) was finished in 2022, while the final piece (Four of Wands) was completed Labor Day, 2024. Each and every card originates from an original acrylic painting, mostly on sturdy wood panels, a few on cotton canvasses. These paintings have names of their own, not tied to tarot cards. So in a way, each of the artworks herein leads a dual life.

Notably, this is the first deck I've created which follows the standard suits. Cups, Swords, Wands, and Pentacles...they're all here. Were you so inclined, you could skip right over this guidebook and go straight to the standard Rider Waite definitions.

That said, I hope you'll give my card meanings a chance.

Major Arcana

The cards of the Major Arcana tell the story of the Fool's Journey. The Fool is card 0. The next twenty cards represent different phases of personal development, individual challenges, spiritual growth, and universal human experiences. The final card, The World, represents the completion of the cycle.

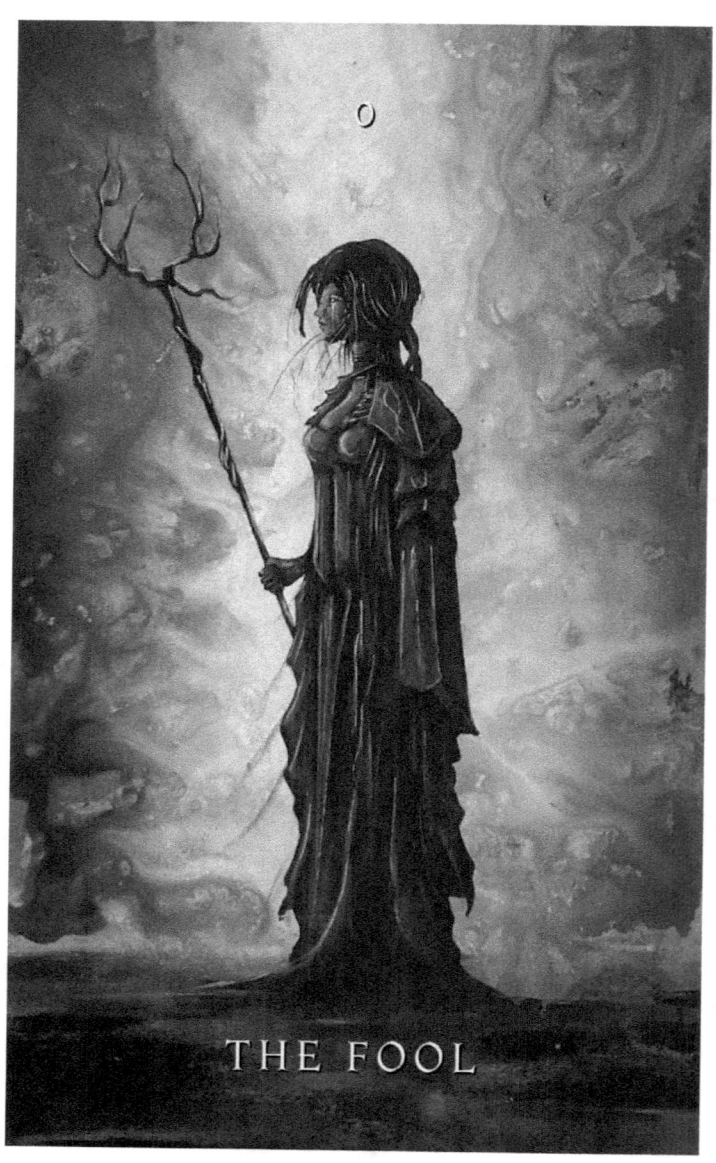

0 The Fool

New Beginnings

It all has to start somewhere, doesn't it?

When you boil down the entirety of the human experience, what you might discover (and be surprised to learn) is that none of us really knows what we're doing. Even the wisest and most successful of us is really just grasping at straws.

We're making it up as we go along.

And we're masters of improvisation.

Think of a child and of their capacity for learning, for fearlessness, and for reckless optimism. If you've pulled The Fool, it might be time for you to channel these traits for your own benefit. This is no time to be inflexible, fearful, or...dare I say it...an adult. How many journeys in life never progress beyond the first few steps, and all because of worry?

This could be one of those, 'What do you have to lose?' moments. So go ahead. Reclaim your childlike innocence. The adventure ahead has the potential to remake everything.

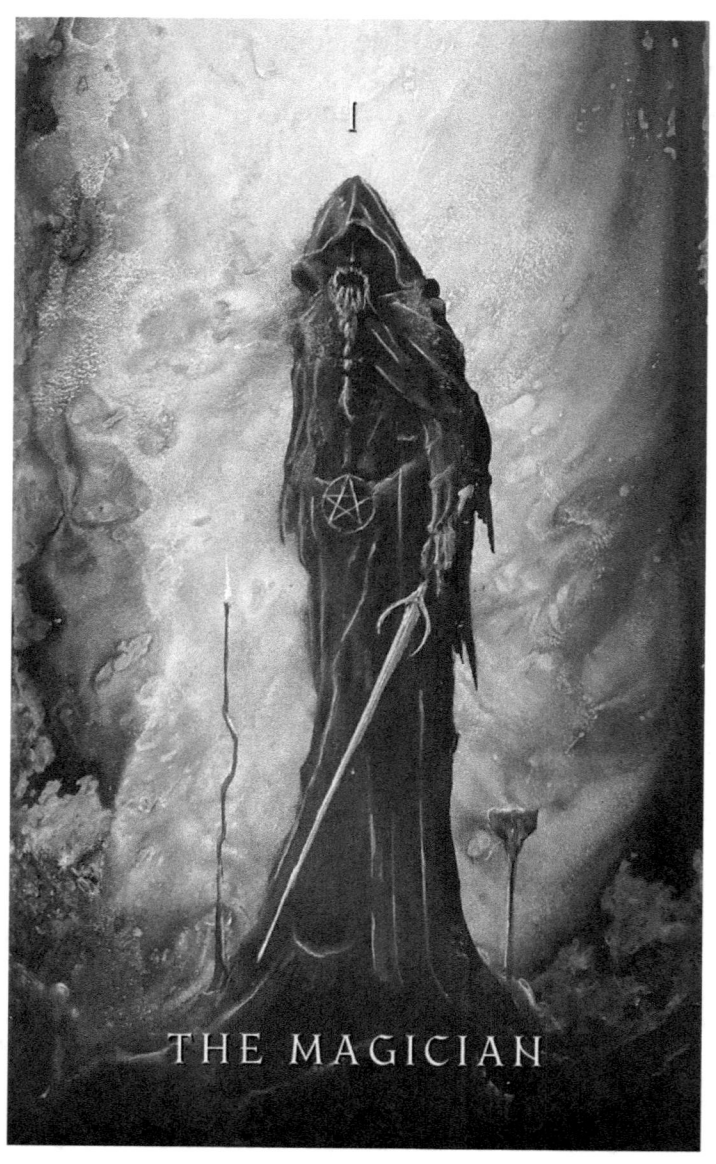

1 The Magician

Create What You Desire

It's not going to land in your lap.

You're going to have to take it.

To wish, to daydream, to hope...these are fanciful things. It's pleasant enough to close your eyes and wonder what might be if you were wealthy, if you were given something you greatly desire, or if the thing you love most loved you back. But daydreams are made of clouds, and rarely do more than dance fluffily across the sky.

Look at yourself. No...do *more* than that. Look *into* yourself, and take stock of all the things at which you are proficient. You probably have more talents, more power, more spiritual resources than you know.

So...if you really want the thing, you're going to have to pick up your sword, your cup, your magic wand, and your pentacle...and you'll need to use these resources to manifest the reality you desire.

Be inspired. Be determined. Recreate your world into a formidable new realm.

Because if you don't do it, who will?

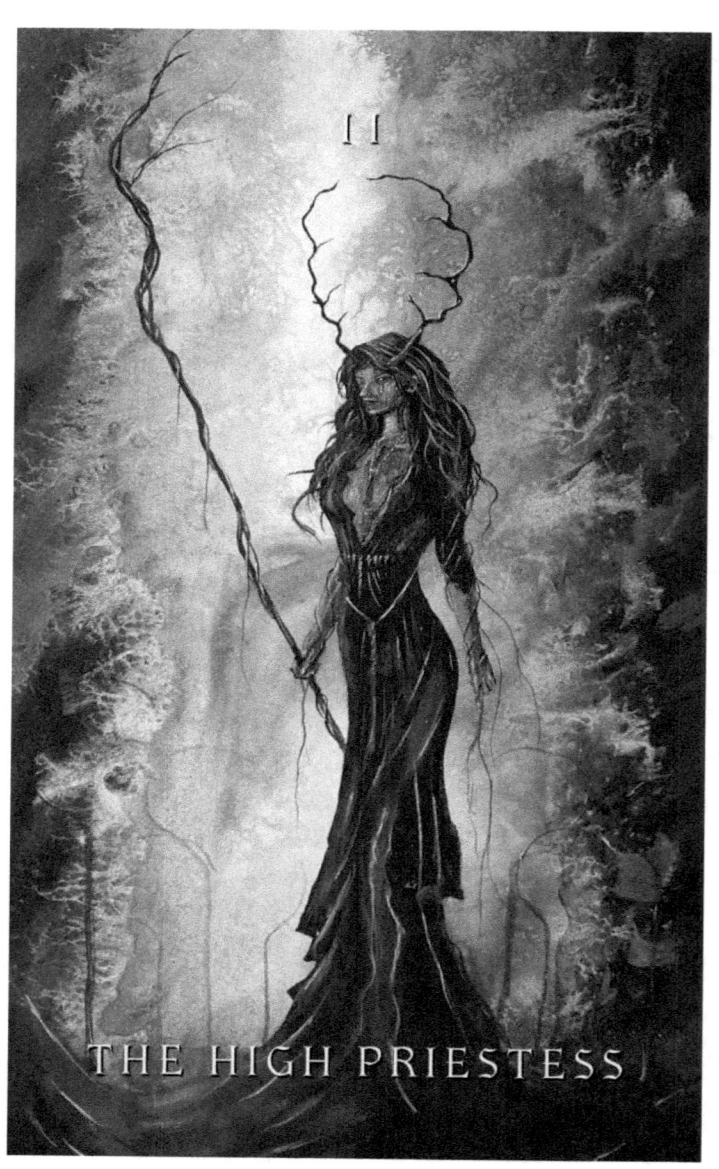

2 The High Priestess

Intuitive Voice

If The Magician's powers are rooted in the physical realm, think of the High Priestess as having mastery over all things spiritual.

If I were you, I'd listen to her.

You know the voice, the one whispering in your ear? It says, 'Stop what you're doing. Listen to me."

And you're familiar with the feeling of knowing, purely by instinct, what's about to happen next.

Think of The High Priestess as your sixth sense. She's your deepest intuition, your spiritual guide, the one who sees all things for what they truly are. If you allow her, she may become your spiritual mediator, aiding you as you wander your way through all the shadowed corners of your innermost thought.

If enlightenment is what you desire, the time is now to open your heart and mind. Trust your gut. Follow your intuition the same as an eager puppy. Clear away the clutter of your mundane thoughts and illuminate the path which lies before you.

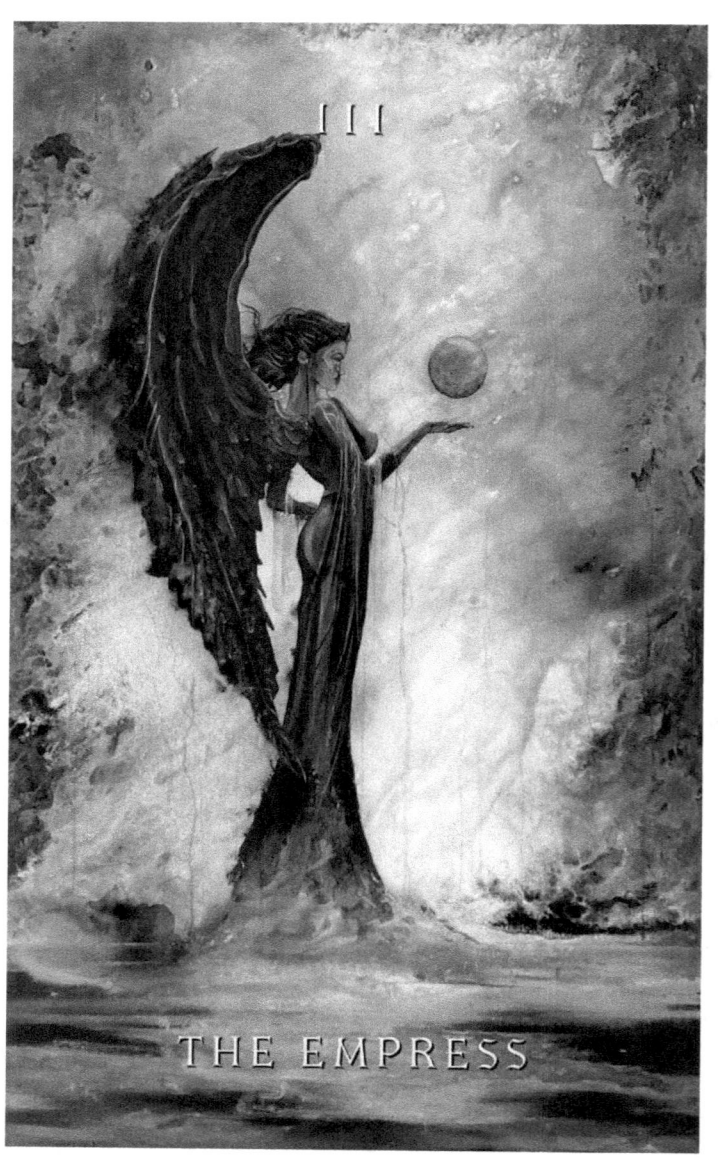

3 The Empress

Creation and Abundance

Think of The Empress as the ultimate Mother Nature. She's both creator and nurturer, powerful in ways other cards can only dream. The Earth and all things in it are her dominion, and yet she holds us in her grasp not with tyranny, but with a mother's careful touch.

The thing about creation is...it's a nebulous concept. And when we speak of nurturing, often our first thoughts meander toward motherhood, toward children and the rearing thereof.

But...

The Empress goes well beyond children. She suggests not only a fertility of body, but of the soul. Yes, pulling her in a tarot spread might mean literal motherhood, but it also implies the creation of art, ideas, abundance, relationships, and ultimately, joy.

It's with passion for these pursuits that you are meant to proceed. Embrace the creation and cultivation of new things in your life. Seek harmony with the natural world.

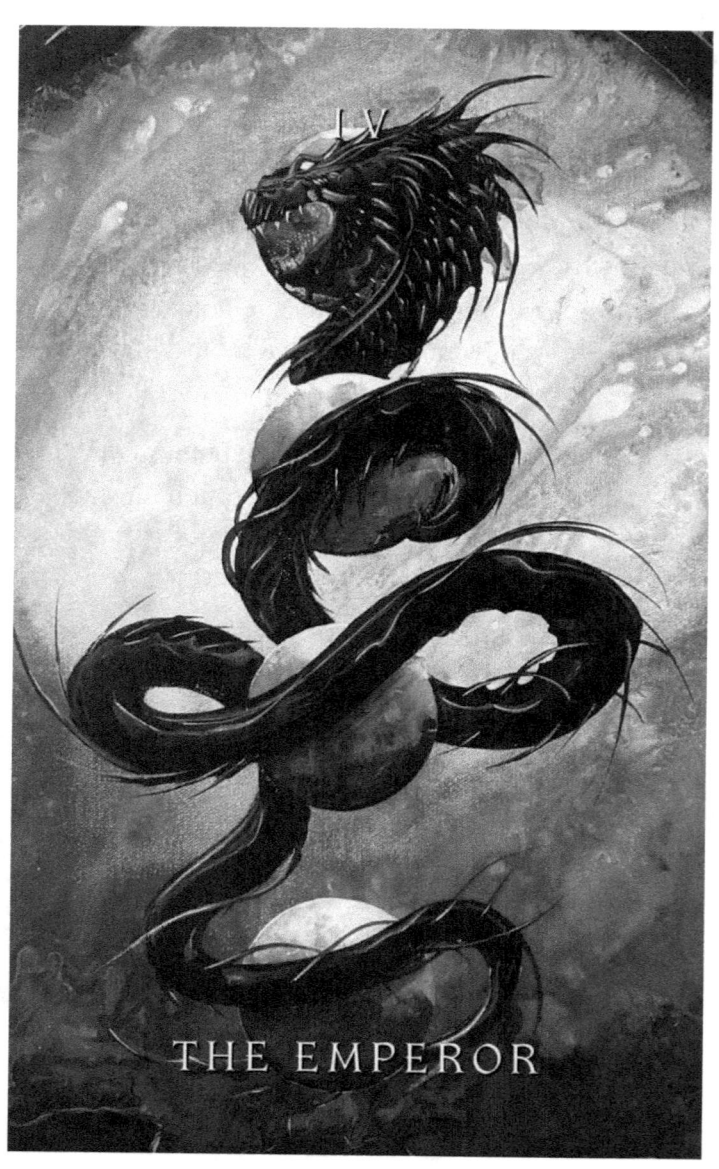

4 The Emperor

Power and Authority

What The Empress creates, The Emperor defends and brings to order.

We are, all of us, meant to be lords of our domain. Our kingdoms may be diminutive, but no less should be our power over them.

Or at least, this is what The Emperor desires. All that we do, all that we touch, it becomes our personal responsibility to protect.

It's a simple matter, really:

Be a steward of all things in your life, not a tyrant.

Craft stable boundaries, not weak shores which incoming waves destroy.

Lead with focus and even-handedness, never reckless self-interest.

The Emperor suggests rationality, decisiveness, and steady leadership. He's meant to set order to the universe which The Empress creates. When you encounter him, you must *become* him.

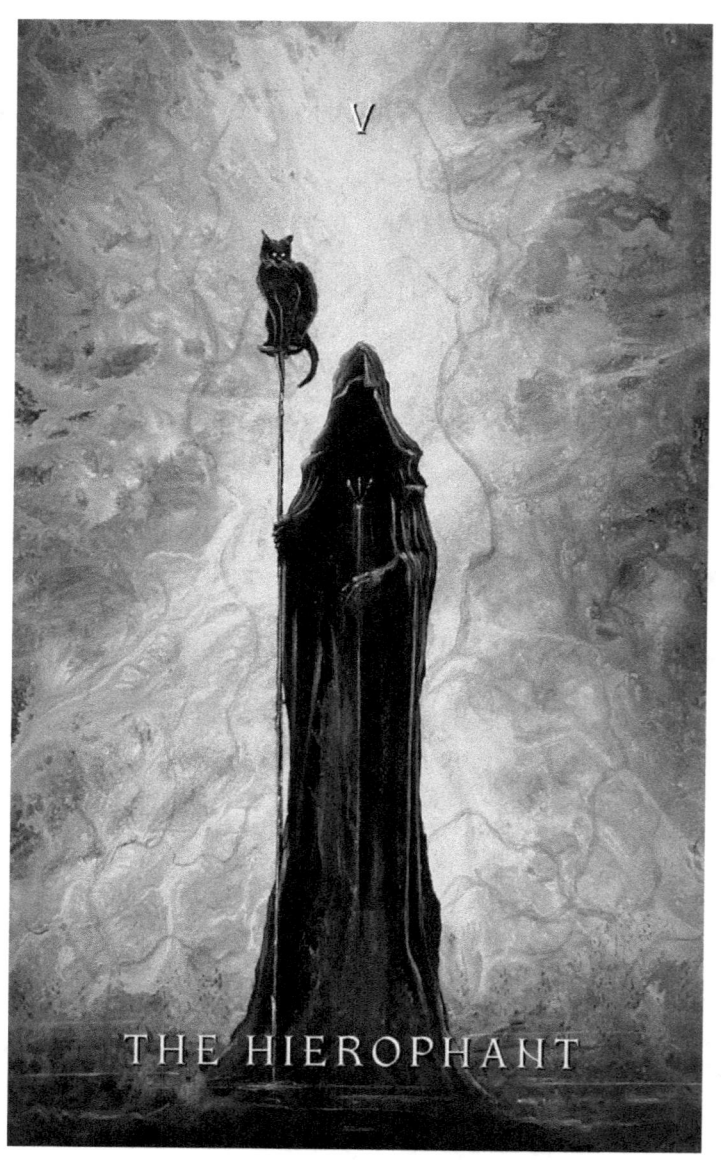

5 The Hierophant

The Traditionalist

One of the ways I prefer to visualize The Hierophant is as a mentor. Imagine, if you will, a village elder, an ancestral presence, the kind of knowledge keeper everyone should be lucky enough to know. If you've ever listened to a grandparent tell tales of their youth while sprinkling in moral lessons (subtle...or not so subtle) then perhaps you've encountered The Hierophant in the flesh.

Hopefully you listened.

Consider this: the ways of the past existed not out of happenstance. If you've ever encountered someone who stubbornly adheres to the rules of yesteryear, who likes none too much the swift progress of younger generations, or is perhaps a bit orthodox in their beliefs, consider that their entire way of living was founded in a world long before your own. There's wisdom to be found in tradition, knowledge to be gained in study.

Before you can master your own way of thinking, seek out a strong foundation. Remember that not all the methods of history are archaic. Spirituality, in particular, transcends the boundary between yesterday and tomorrow. If you are to build your character, you must first become a willing student.

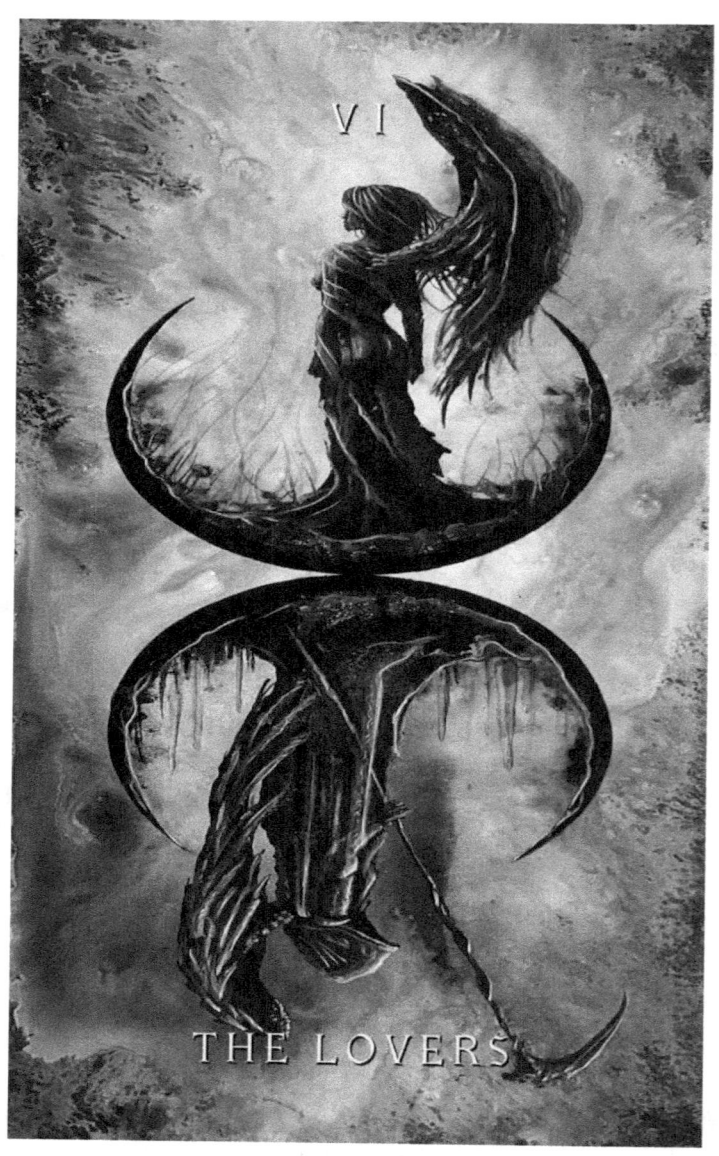

6 The Lovers

Harmony, Relationships

Ah, love...

It wears many masks, arrives in a variety of packaging, and surely represents our purest state of vulnerability.

Love is about honesty.

About trust.

About allowing someone else into your heart without barriers to entry.

We're not speaking only of romantic love, of course. Whether the connection you've made (or are about to make) is a life-partner, a friend, or a family member, your goal should be to remain authentic. Let this person with whom you've bonded perceive you as your truest self. After all, this is the only way you'll know your love is true.

It's unfiltered. It's honest, even brutally at times.

Love is also about choices. And consequences. To love another (and to love yourself) you must know yourself. You must choose who you are and who you want to be, and co-exist with all that will come of these choices. Seek unity within yourself – find harmony with those you've admitted into your heart.

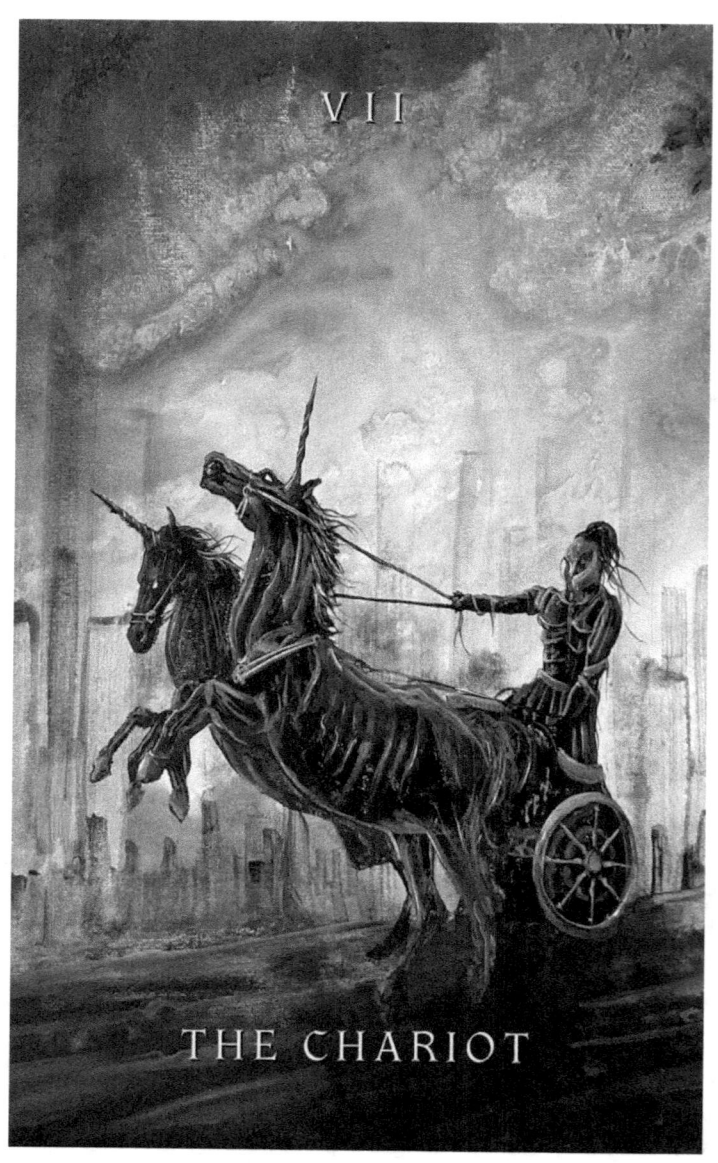

7 The Chariot

Force of Will

Be encouraged by this singular thought:

Through determination, willpower, and a never-say-die attitude, you can and will conquer everything.

Oh...it won't be easy. There will be potholes, speedbumps, and other obstacles on the journey ahead (whether a literal journey or a spiritual voyage.) To overcome these, you'll need to be unstoppable. And if you find yourself wanting to waver, you'll need to ask yourself, 'Did I really want this in the first place?'

Think of the momentum gained with The Lovers card. You've decided who you are and what you want to be, and now that you've arrived at The Chariot, you'll need to achieve your desires through direct and confident physical action.

What to avoid?

Passivity

Self-doubt

Corner-cutting

This moment is a test. Push forward hard enough, and you will pass.

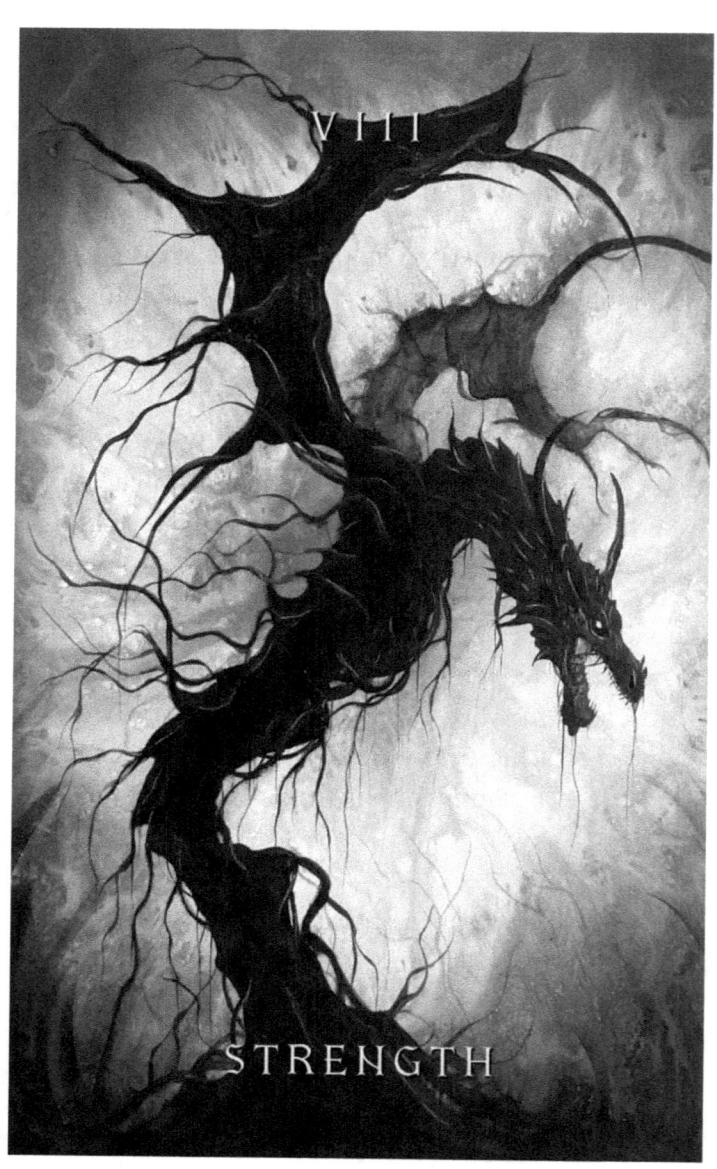

8 Strength

Power of the Mind

Inside all of us, a dragon slumbers.

Others might not see it. Those around you might look at you and believe you are soft, gentle, or emotionally fragile.

All your dragon awaits is the right catalyst to awaken.

If The Chariot is all about pure physical action and raw, untamed willpower, Strength is about harnessing the power of your innermost self. Explosive, uncontrolled emotions may have undermined you in the past, but this moment is yours to remain composed, to overcome fear, and to move forward for the better good of yourself and others.

Should you avoid your emotions? No. You must tame them and turn them into something which benefits you. Look closely at your instincts and gut reactions. Do they serve you? Or do they hinder you?

Remember these lessons:

Vulnerability is not weakness.

All that bends does not break.

Love is the greatest strength you can possess.

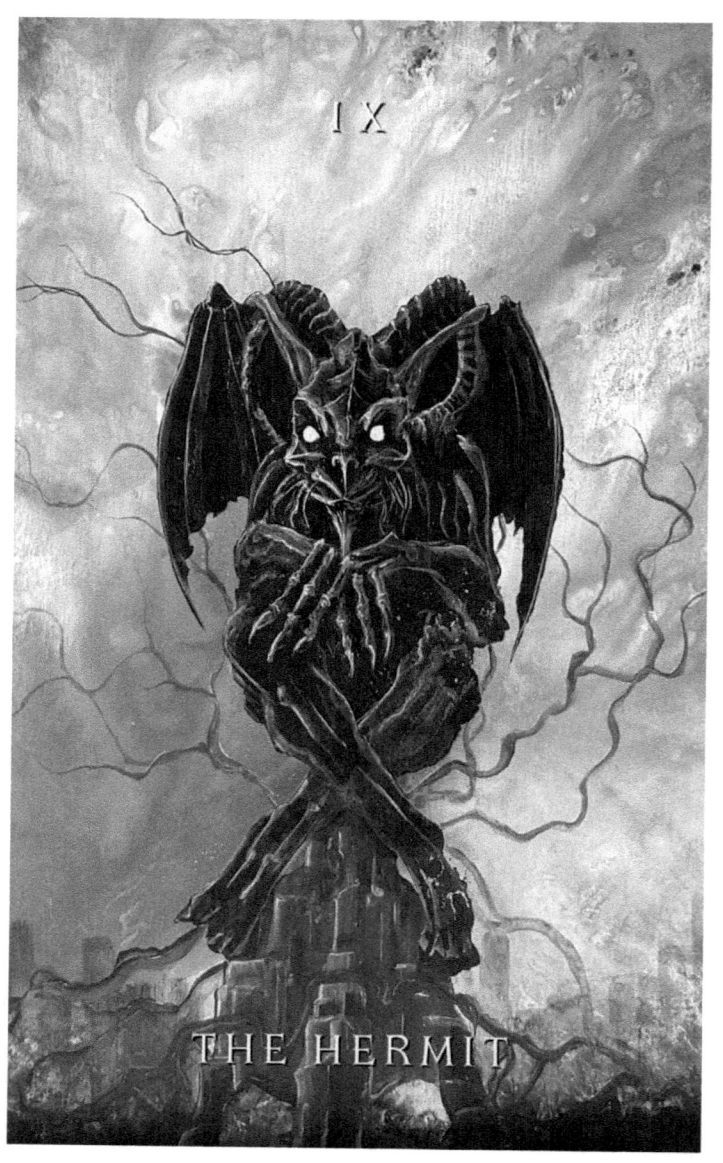

9 The Hermit

Meditation. Self-Reflection

To truly know yourself...

You must *be* yourself.

...*by* yourself.

Consider this – the path to self-awareness is forged through solitude. Not in body or location, but in mind and spirit. Looked at in a literal sense, The Hermit suggests fleeing to a deep, dark cave and existing in abject, lonely oneness. But really what it means is honest self-examination. Remove the world's noise, close off the opinions of others, and achieve self-truth.

The Hermit's arrival means you are to take this role of self-reflection all alone.

Or...it could suggest that someone else, a mentor, teacher, or an unselfish individual has assumed the role of faithful guide in your life.

When I think of true Hermit energy, I don't dwell so much on withdrawing from the world. Rather, I prefer to take time (every day, if possible) to consider what I'm doing. Are my actions aligning with who I really am? Is this, whatever I'm doing in the moment, a reflection of who I truly want to be?

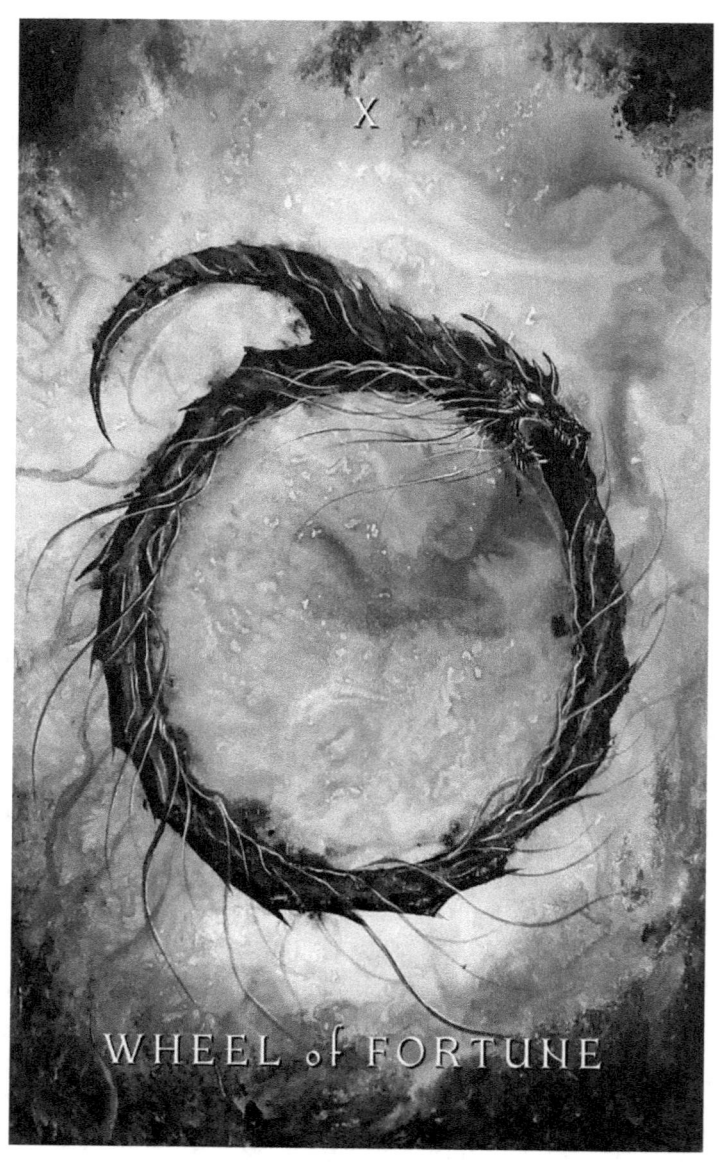

10 Wheel of Fortune

Beginnings and Endings

Reaching the mountaintop...

...usually a pleasant myth.

If you've ever achieved something great...or sunken to some desperate low, you know these things are temporary. The ephemeral nature of joy and sorrow, of success and failure, they compose the circular rhythm of our lives. Ups and downs, so to speak, are entirely natural phenomena, and are not to be feared.

I'm willing to wager that if you took inventory of your life at this very moment, and if you mapped your position on the path to your next life goal, you would recognize the circular motion of things. Ideas become goals. Goals become movement. Movement becomes achievement, for better or worse.

What then does achievement become? Most likely, more ideas. And so the wheel forever turns.

If you're struggling, know that continuing on the wheel will lead you toward something better. And if things are smooth sailing, perhaps you're due for a new challenge to arrive. The key is to anticipate these changes, to pivot and adjust with the knowledge that nothing lasts forever, and that endings are merely beginnings in disguise.

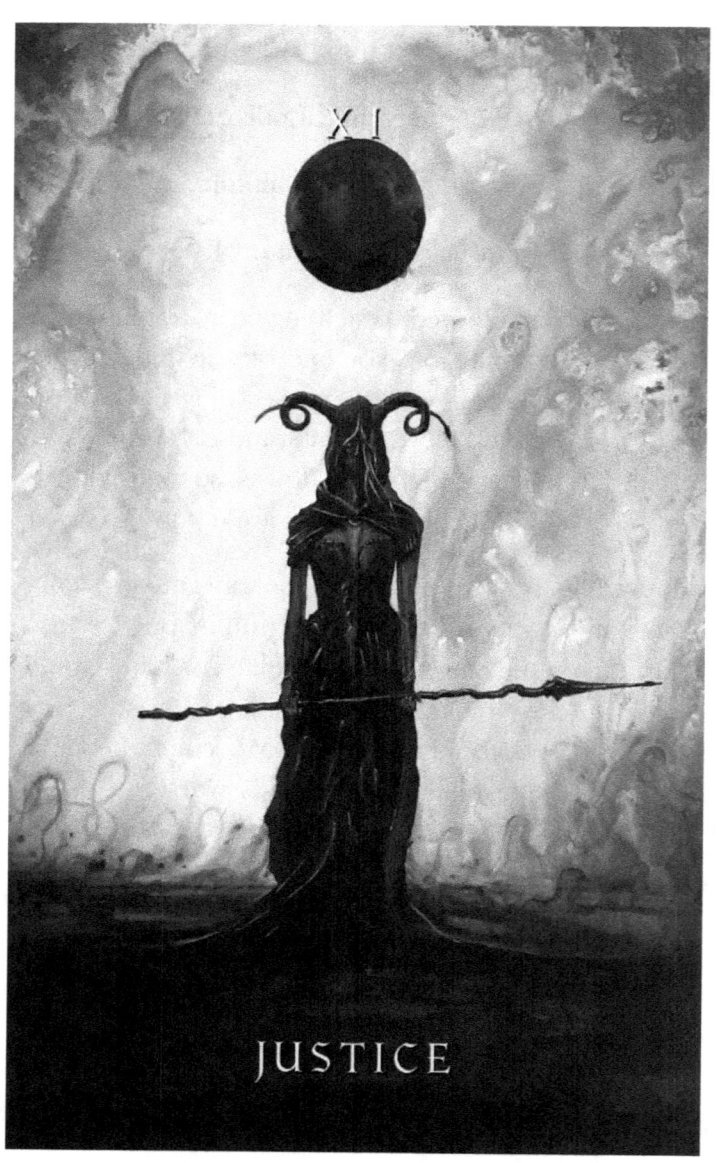

11 Justice

Consequence

One day, it'll all come crashing down...

Think of the Justice card as life's big red warning sign. Something ill has happened. For there to be Justice in your tarot spread, there must first have been an *injustice.*

There's been a lie.

A secret kept.

A dark deed performed in the shadows.

And now comeuppance is inevitable.

Moreover, you or someone you love may have *self-inflicted* this injury. Remember that the worst lies are those we tell ourselves, and the deepest wounds are those we wreak upon our own soul. This injustice may have been inflicted *upon* you...or perhaps it was perpetrated *by* you.

Fortunately, Justice isn't strictly about punishment. It's about acceptance, about righting wrongs, about honesty and truth. Yes, there will be consequences, but the twin evils of shame and guilt can be undone. Better to make it right than to carry a heavy burden to the end of your days.

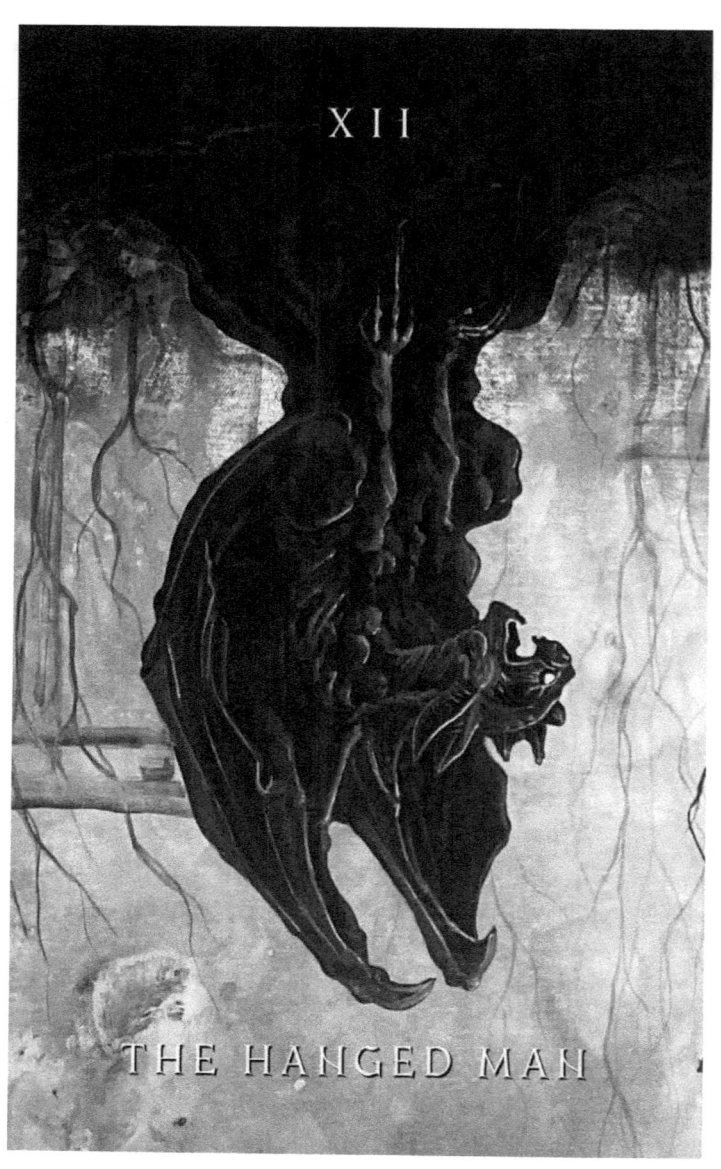

12 The Hanged Man

The Pause Button

Stop. Go no further.

We are not meant to be machines.

Every day of our lives is not supposed to look the same.

When the routines and habits of your existence begin to feel monotonous or more like a prison than a healthy way of living, this is the right moment for Hanged Man energy. Just look at him, hung eternally in place, suspended in stillness.

He's pondering change.

He's contemplating all the opportunities missed.

His world has ground to a momentary halt, and for good reason.

In this quiet moment, consider yourself. Look at your relationships, your career, and all the motion to which you are bound in your everyday life. Have you missed out on anything? Is something far from what it could be? Now is the time to reflect on the river of your life, and to remove the stones which impede your flow. Hear what your heart desires, and remind yourself to live with a purpose that reflects this desire.

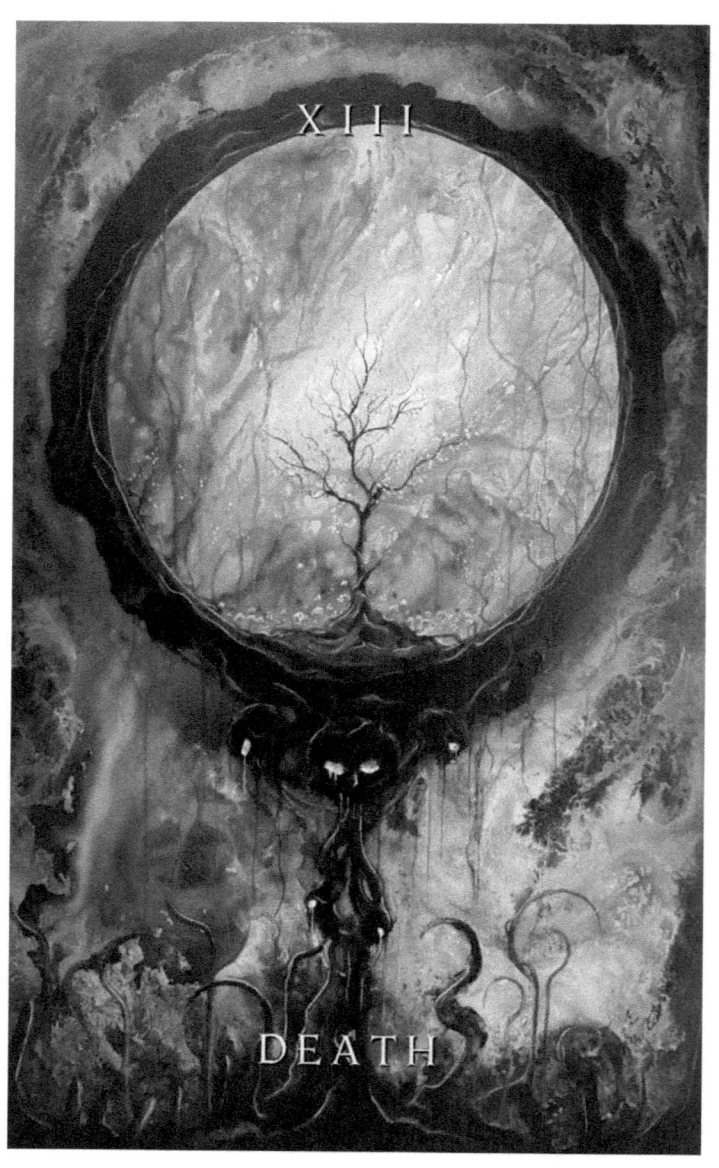

13 Death

Transformation

Uh oh...

It's the card we all love to fear.

First, let's clear away any lingering anxiety. Death, in this context, rarely means physical expiration. It's about powerful change, and the transition to a new way of life on the other side.

Think of Death as your spiritual resurrection. Parts of your life, small and huge, will inevitably meet their end. Many things will flutter away, some never returning, others wandering back into your awareness utterly changed from what they once were.

This is perfectly natural. Death, especially in a non-literal sense, is a necessary event. Parts of your life that are no longer healthy or useful must wither. New petals and leaves must burst into life within you.

It's true. It may be painful. The hardest part of change is accepting that what once was...will no longer be. Letting go of yesterday and embracing the upheaval of tomorrow hurts, but is ultimately rewarding. The less you resist the notion of inevitable transformation, the sooner you can embrace the newest version of yourself.

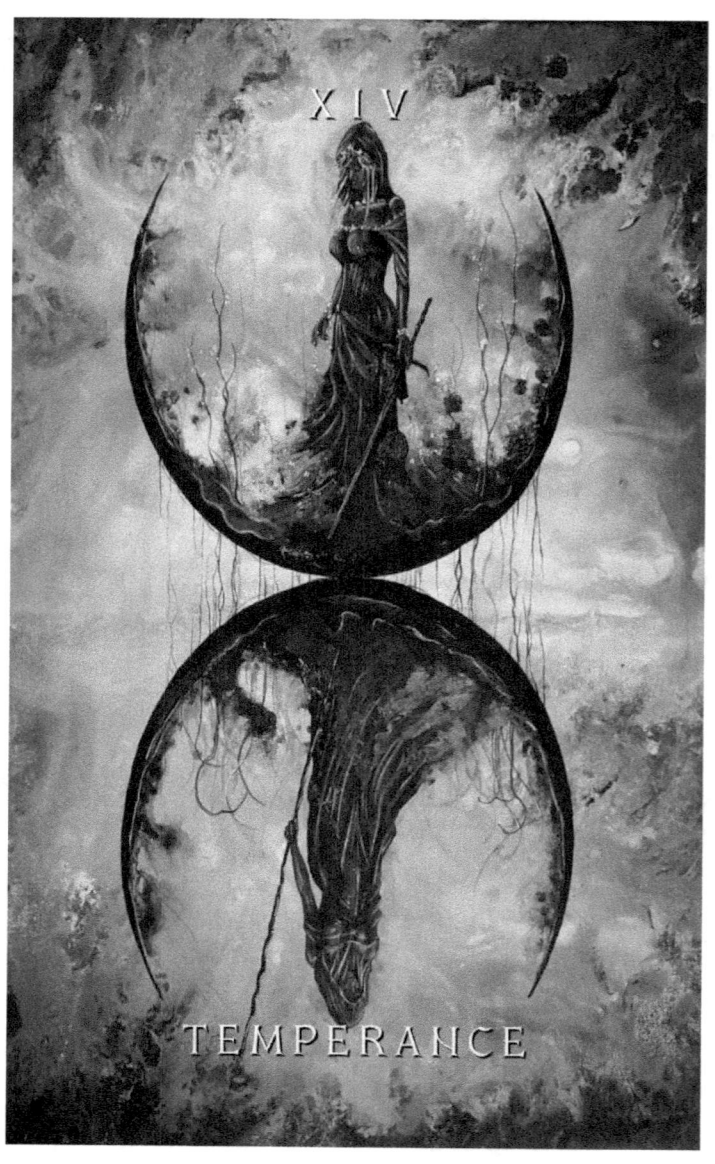

14 Temperance

Balance. Patience

Everything you consume, do so in moderation.

The meaning of Temperance could probably end with this one simple reminder, but let's take it deeper.

To find true inner peace, you must first discover a healthy balance of all the elements in your life. This means not only balance within your relationships, your job, and your emotions, but also with your food, spending habits, and all of your physical pursuits.

Indulge too much in something, and it will haunt you.

Neglect your body or deny yourself some needed thing, and you will pay the dearest price.

Think of Temperance in terms of the mantra, 'As above, so below.' What you do with your body will be reflected in your soul. If you seek balance in your daily existence and exercise self-control over all that you do, your mind and spirit will be grateful.

For your body, take what you need, but no more.

For your mind, exercise patience, calm, and good judgement.

For your soul, seek emotional balance.

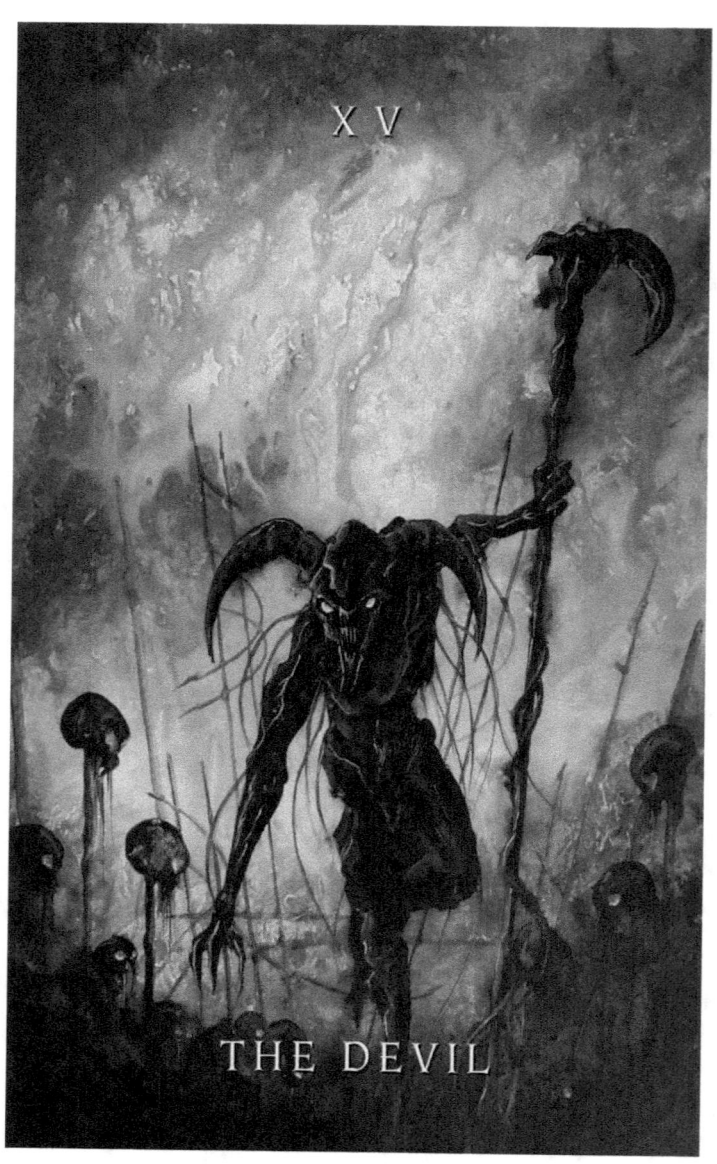

15 The Devil

Imprisonment

Everything we learned about Temperence, think of The Devil as the opposite.

Things that might cause this unpleasant fellow to appear in your tarot spread:

Your thoughts have become intrusive, disruptive, maybe even obsessive.

You want little to do with consuming in moderation.

You seek instant gratification.

You believe you're in control of your life, but it's an illusion.

First things first. It's time to acknowledge that some negative influence has a hold over you.

Next, be *illuminated.*

Here's the thing – The Devil can only hold sway over you if you allow it. Without your consent, he has no power. Just as you may have invited dark influences into your life, you can uninvite them just as swiftly.

The walls of your prison are illusory. Once you recognize your ability to leave, to break bad patterns, and to crush your addictions, you can simply walk free without a moment's fear.

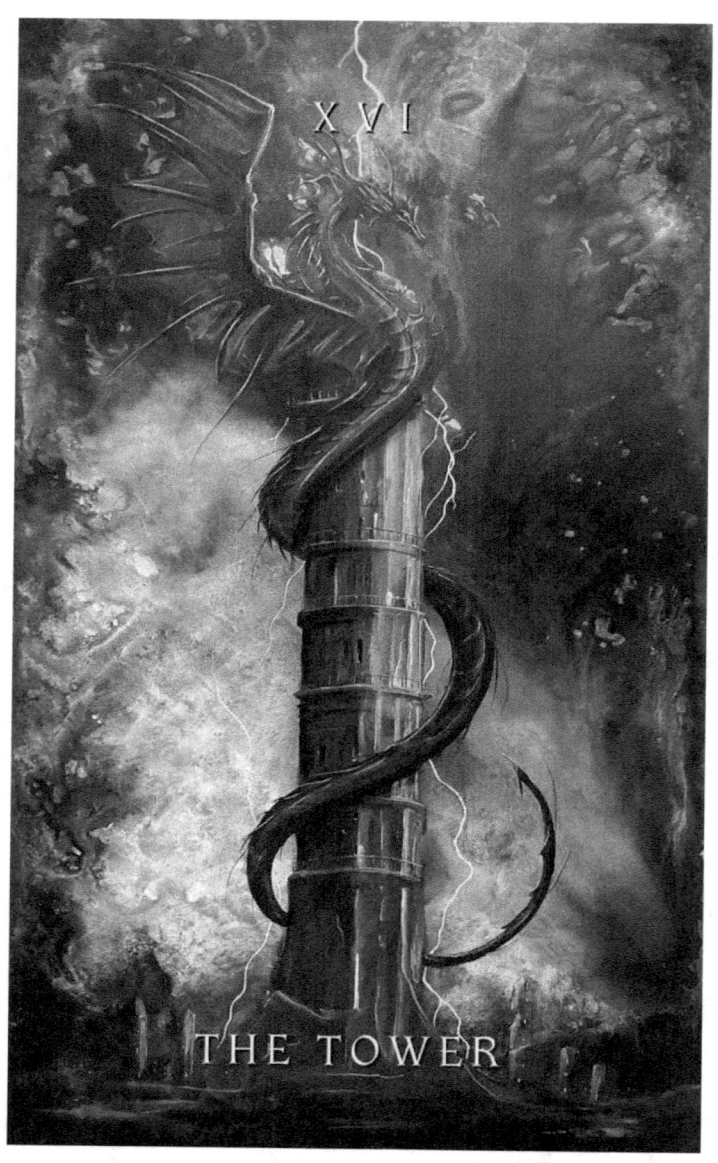

16 The Tower

The Inevitable Fall

Here we go...

The deep breath before the plunge...

All towers will crumble. All structures, no matter how powerful, must meet their demise.

So it goes with everything, both physical and spiritual.

You may think the foundation of *you* is unbreakable, but it's never quite true. A few unexpected cracks in the foundation of your life, and down it all will tumble. Comfort zones, future plans, the pleasant veil you've tugged over your eyes...they're ephemeral. Great upheaval is coming, and you'd best accept it and be prepared for the change.

It's okay to be afraid when The Tower falls. When it all comes crashing down, it's likely you'll endure a great deal of insecurity. And yet, this could be the beginning of something newer and better. In this moment, the opportunity will arise to build a stronger foundation. All the secrets, cracks, and weaknesses of your old life will be cast down and exposed. This is a good thing. The Tower fell for a reason. Now is your chance to build a better one.

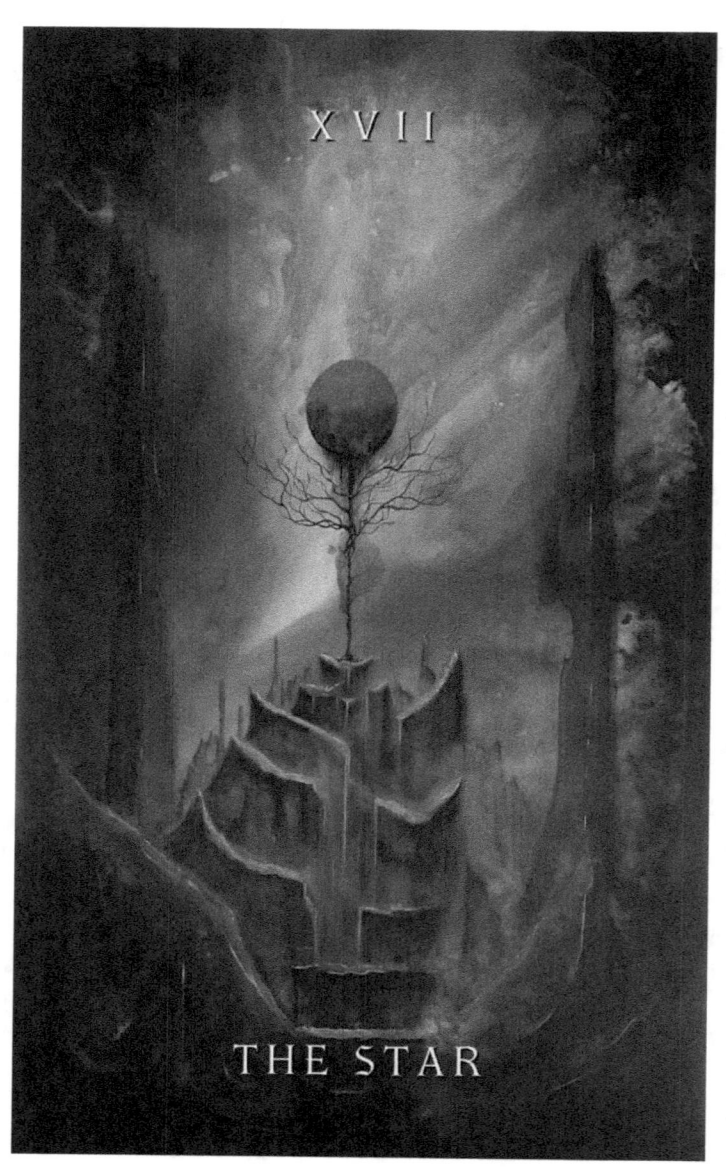

17 The Star

Rebuilding. Renewal

The Tower has fallen, and you are left to wander amid the broken pathways of your previous life.

Have hope. The Star shines brightly.

Look upon The Star as a light at tunnel's end. Like a beacon when hope dwindles, it's also a symbol meant to remind you of your strength. Many things deep inside you which haven't yet been tapped will now awaken. All of us hold just beneath our surface a hidden reservoir of energy. Seek this energy and draw upon it. It's the very stuff of life.

Now is the time to tap into your inner resilience. When life leaves you feeling broken, alone, and world-weary, these are the moments to show your true character.

Too often, we give up just moments from reaching our dreams. Only those of us who persist despite all obstacles will break through. This is not the time for quitting.

This is your hour of renewal.

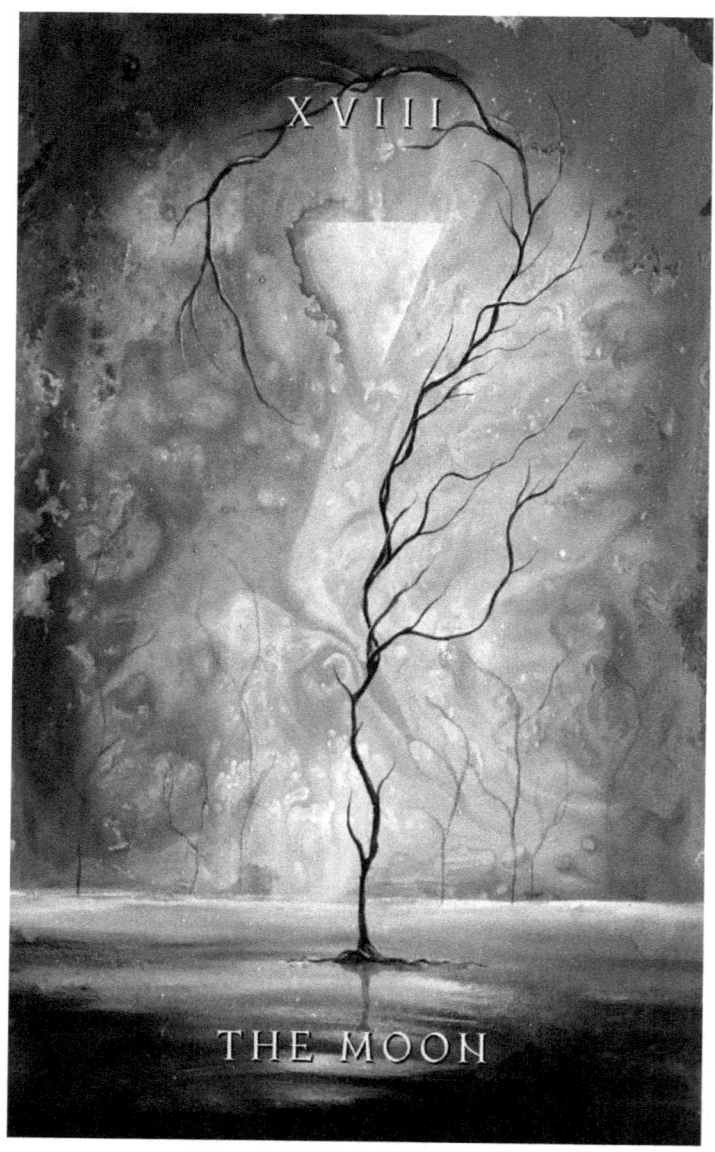

18 The Moon

Illusions

Nothing is as it seems.

I like to think of The Moon as the great revealer. Like a lantern floating in the night sky, its serene light illuminates truth, dispels shadow, and serves as a guide through the dark machinery of the world around us.

The Moon reminds us:

The worst lies are those we tell to ourselves.

The most dangerous fears are those we choose not to face.

The enemy of truth is false perception.

Truth is, most of us are pushed through our lives by forces we do not fully comprehend. We follow half-truths, unclear visions, and outright illusions toward the promise of tomorrow, and we don't always know why. When The Moon arrives, it signals a moment of clarity is at hand. Allow its light to shine upon your subconscious. Trust not your eyes and ears, but rather follow your deepest intuition. Be wary of fear and self-deception. These things should not control you. Follow what is true, not what is wished-for.

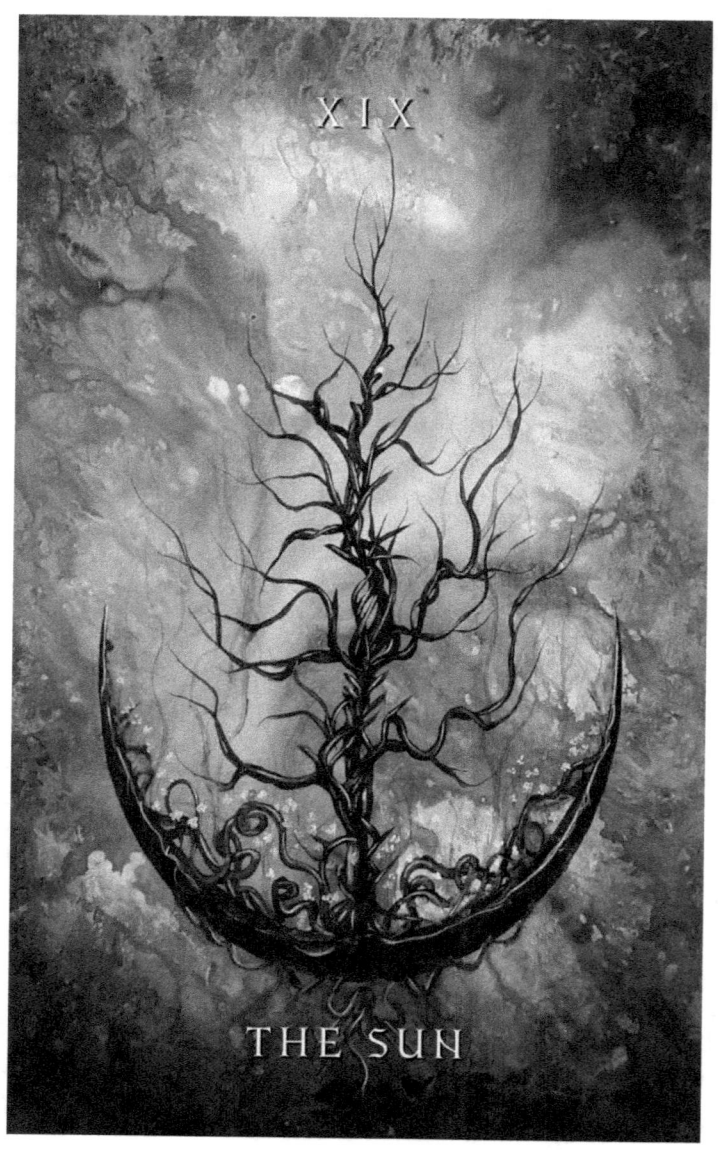

19 The Sun

The Happiest Card

Today could be a good one.

If not right this very instant, then very soon you will reach a sublime moment. All the radiance of The Sun is destined to shine upon you, delivering optimism, renewal, and pure, unadulterated joy.

These moments are rare, and should be treasured.

If ever there were a time to cut loose and loudly express yourself, this is it. Abundance of some kind (spiritual, physical, or even financial) is soon to cross your path. All you need to do is accept it. If The Moon is the revealer, think of The Sun as the great rekindler.

This is the perfect moment to:

Make important life decisions

Throw aside your previous inhibitions

Embrace your creative side

For one shining moment, you may feel unstoppable. If so, it's because you *ARE.*

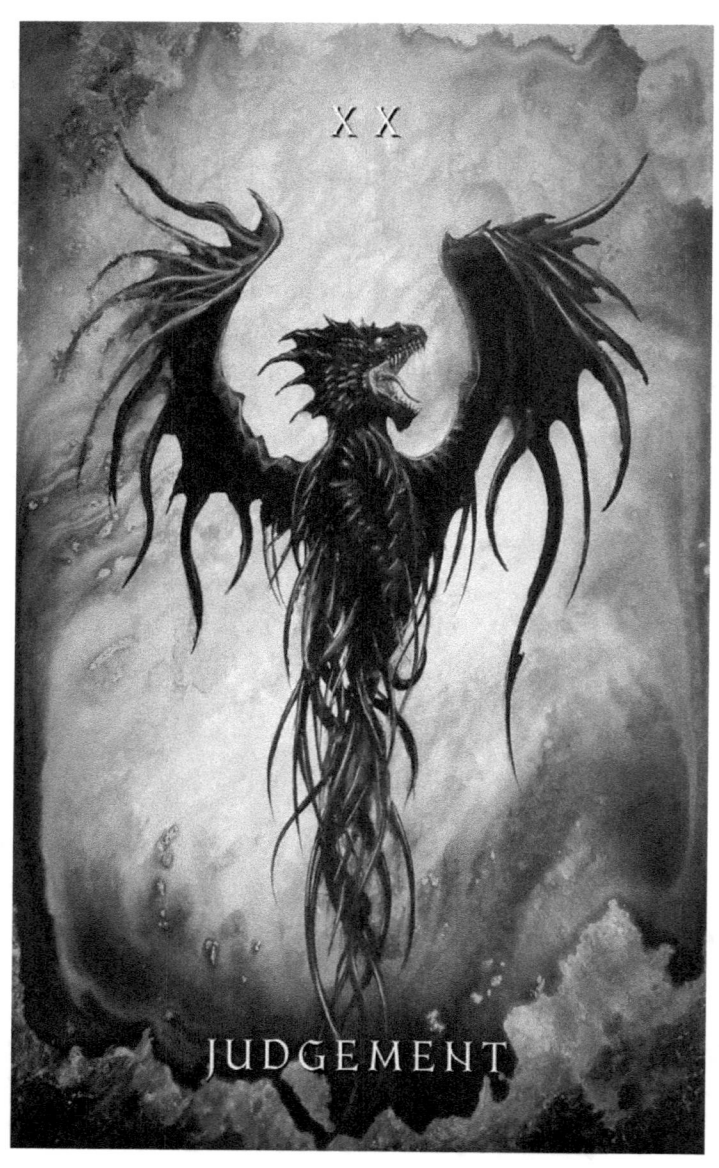

20 Judgement

Deep Reflection

Judgement...the final step before The World.

If we view the Major Arcana as a pathway through peril and triumph before reaching the end of a great journey, then Judgement should be considered your final moment of self-reflection. If this card rests before your eyes, it signals that before you arrive at your promised end, you must breathe deeply and consider yourself.

There are consequences to success, the same as for failure. Before ascension, Judgement desires that you know yourself, that you are honest and authentic when you look into the mirror, and that the goal for which you strive is something you really, truly desire.

For the moment, shed any lingering concerns for the past. Instead, consider the emotions, experiences, and desires which compose the entire sum of *you*.

Are you truly who you believe yourself to be?

Do your actions reflect the person you desire to be?

Are you ready for the journey's end, and the beginning of something new?

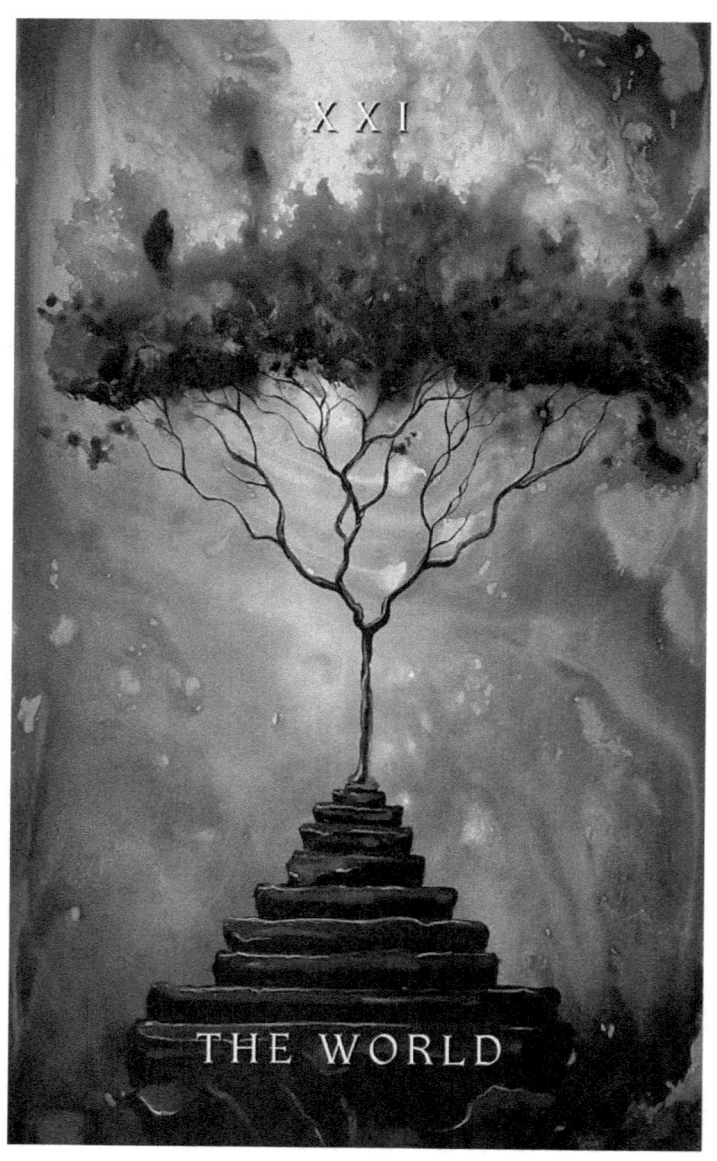

21 The World

The Circle Complete

How often do we get to bask in the light of an accomplishment, a goal reached, or a rare achievement?

A handful of times in our lives.

When you reach the pinnacle of The World, it's best not to think of it as an ending. It's time to celebrate, for certain. One journey is complete, and it's worth savoring the moment. But this isn't the end of the road. The journey will continue. Soon, you'll pack up everything you've learned, all your experience, growth, and success...

...and you'll begin again as The Fool.

For now, enjoy the mountaintop view. A vast ocean of possibility will soon open up before you. New roads, new experiences...the mists will part and reveal a wide realm of opportunity.

Release yourself from all things of the past which hindered you. Remember that your road to success goes on into infinity.

Minor Arcana

The Minor Arcana represents everyday themes and aspects of daily life. It consists of four suits. Here, in Dark Fantasy Tarot, the four suits are: Wands, Cups, Swords, and Pentacles, which are identical to traditional tarot.

There are four court cards in each suit: Page, Knight, Queen, and King. These four cards can represent your different personality traits and behavioral patterns during the different stages of your life. They may also represent actual people who are in your life now, have been in your life in the past, or will be in your life in the future.

Wands

The suit of Wands represents ideas, personal inspiration, ambition, and creative passion. It corresponds to the element of fire. The theme of Wands is all about movement, energy, and primal spirituality.

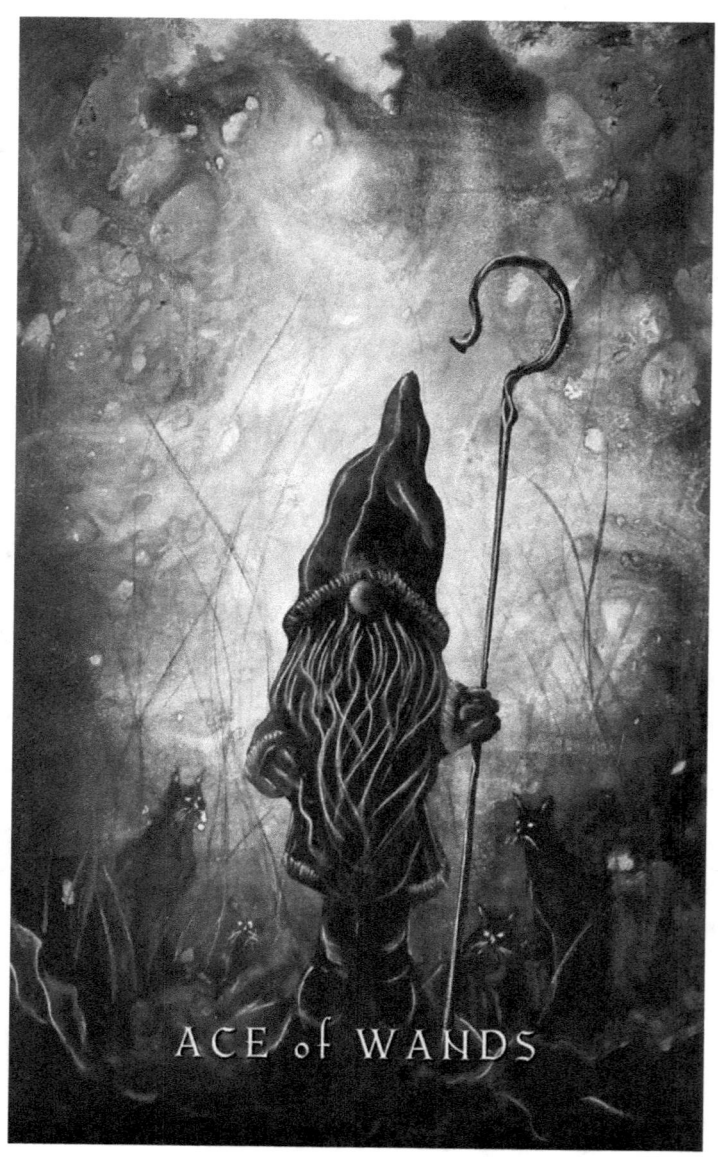

Ace of Wands

Inspiration

I like to think of the Aces as The Fools of the Minor Arcana. They bring something new and fresh to the table. They represent the potential for new beginnings. In this case, the Ace of Wands is an awakening, a tap on your sleeping shoulder. Perhaps you've been daydreaming of an idea to change your life. Or maybe the embers of a passion from long ago stir within your heart.

Listen to your dreams.

Fan those embers.

Now is the time to choose where your time and energy will be directed. There's an opportunity here, whether large or small. There's a choice to be made involving a new project, a job, or perhaps even a romantic tryst. Remember that Wands are all about movement and creativity. This is no time to remain static or to allow doubt to hold you back.

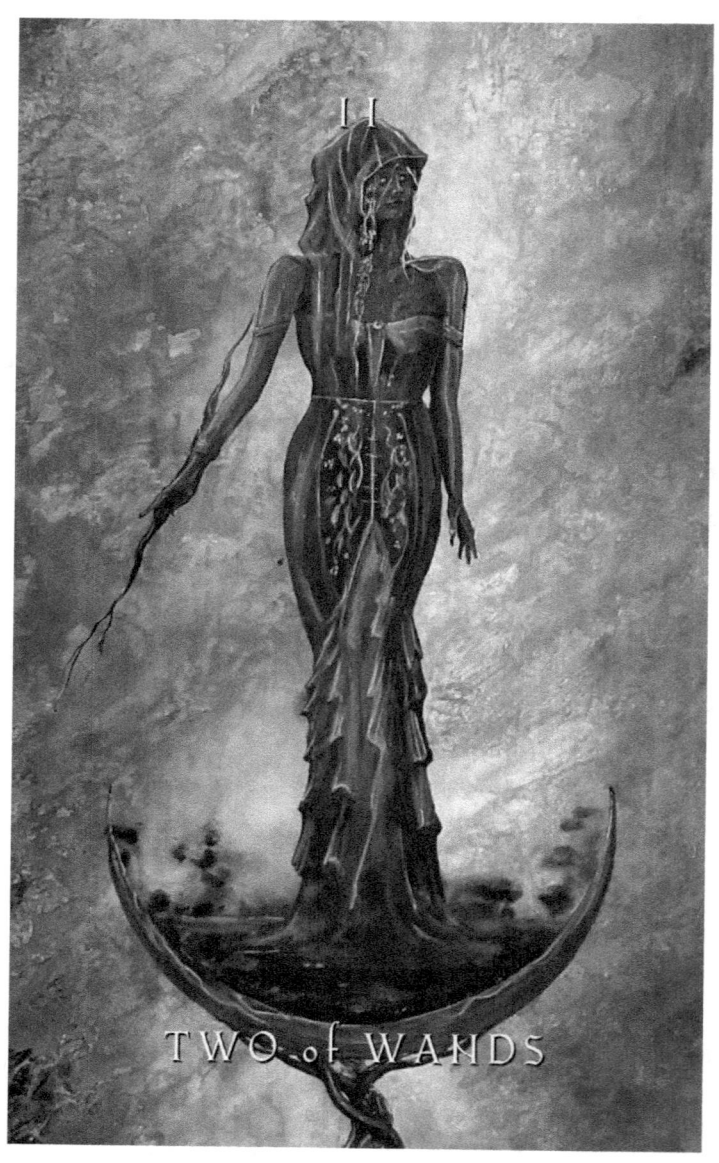

Two of Wands

Life Strategy

This is no time to walk blindly into the fog of tomorrow.

This is your moment to craft a plan.

The Two of Wands desires good things, but only if nurtured with focus, clarity, and positive intent. You've probably noticed by now the large number of tarot cards which call upon you to embrace your intuition, to follow your instincts.

This isn't one of those moments.

The things you desire can be had, but there is a price. As you progress toward your next goal in life, the Two of Wands suggests deep preparation, practicality, and pragmatism. Don't let these efforts temper or reduce your enthusiasm. Rather, let your focus become your shield. Just because you're carefully crafting your future ambitions doesn't mean you can't greet them with excitement.

Plan today. Succeed tomorrow.

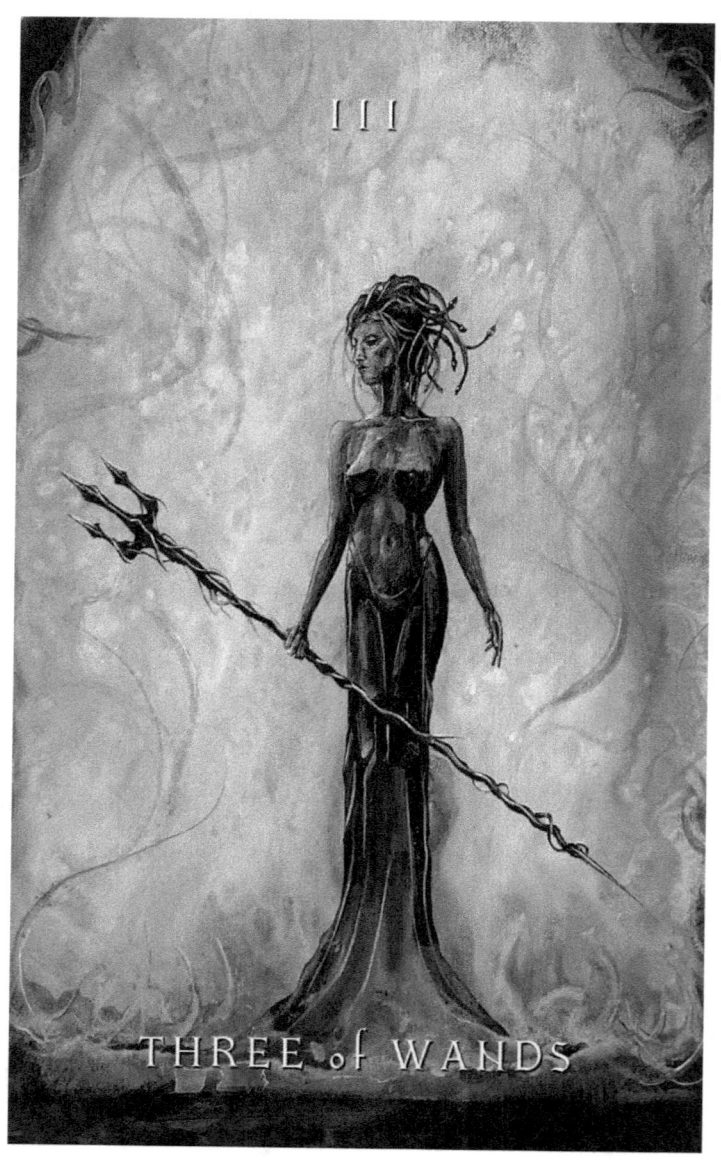

Three of Wands

Widening Horizons

Sometimes, comfort zones are for cowards.
There...it's been said.
You say you desire good things for yourself.
You say you want to grow, to learn, to travel, and to reach your potential.
Well...
Pick up your wand (or trident) and puncture the bubble in which you've been living.
The Three of Wands is all about expanding your mind, body, and soul. It's time to learn that skill for which you've been pining, to book that journey you've been putting off, and to look beyond the things which historically have limited you.
If a challenge lies before you, and if you're afraid (especially if you're afraid) now is the moment to overcome it. Nothing good will come of waiting. Go forth and fear no darkness.

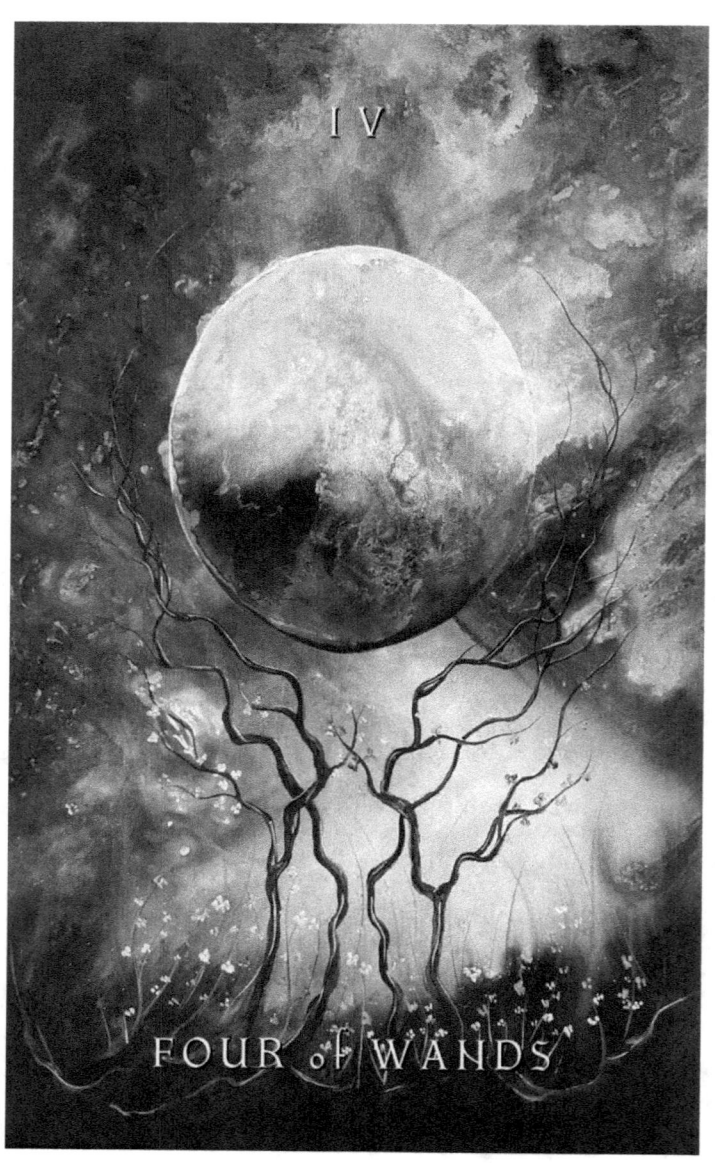

Four of Wands

A Brief Respite

With wise planning, moving beyond your comfort zones, and successful manifestation of your desires, you have reached an important milestone. It's time to bask in the glow.

The Four of Wands represents stability, balance, and perhaps even joy. Take time to savor what you have achieved. Now would be a good moment to spend time with friends, loved ones, and return to the place you call home. A moment of rest and reflection is owed you.

It's possible you may find yourself basking alone. Your successes could be of a highly personal nature, or it could be that you feel your achievements have gone unnoticed by others. Fear not. Reach upward into yourself, and acknowledge your successes privately.

Whether alone or in the company of others, your growth is real and genuine. Never forget this.

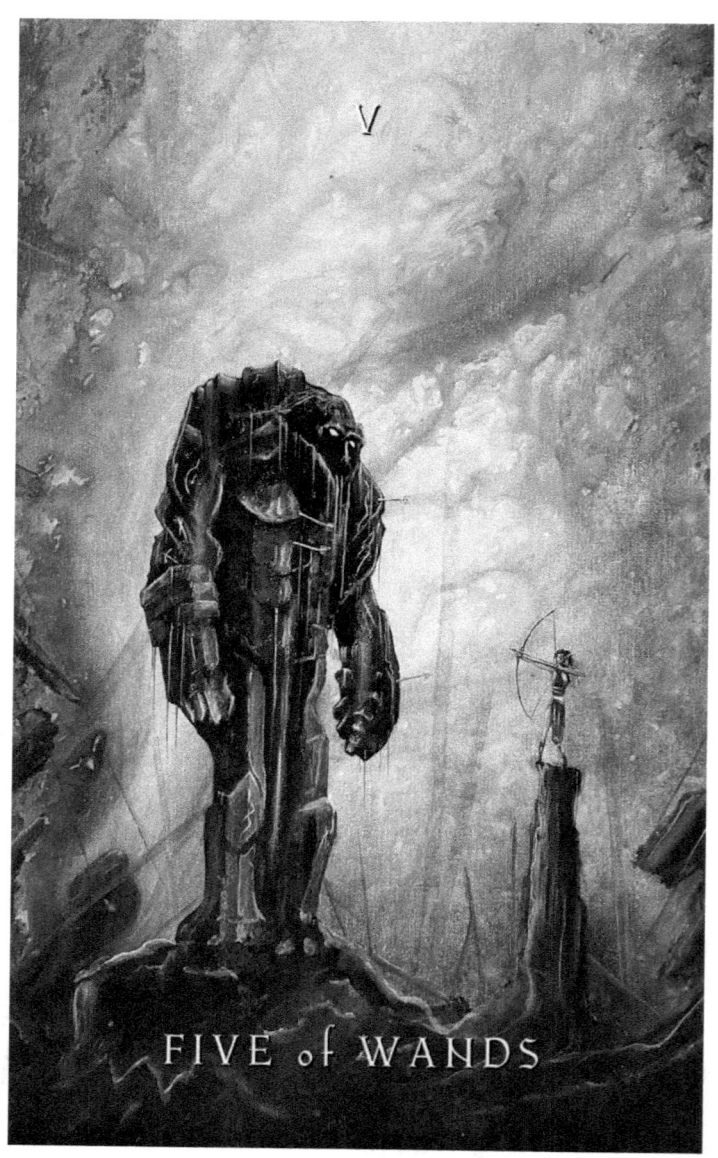

Five of Wands

The Nemesis

There comes a time when you may discover that you've climbed too high...

...in the eyes of others.

The not-so-subtle interpretation of the Five of Wands is that you are destined for conflict, specifically with another person. Be wary. It could be a case of simple competitive rivalry, or it could sink into open conflict, envy, or even that worst of all emotions, *jealousy*. These tensions might brew quietly, like simmering broth beneath a covered pot.

Or they could be explosive.

First and foremost, your goal should be to identify the source of conflict. Resolution is better than warfare, but if it's too late for diplomacy or quiet tact, you'll need to rise above it. Communicate with your rival(s), but don't capitulate. Grow and learn, but do not allow yourself to be manipulated.

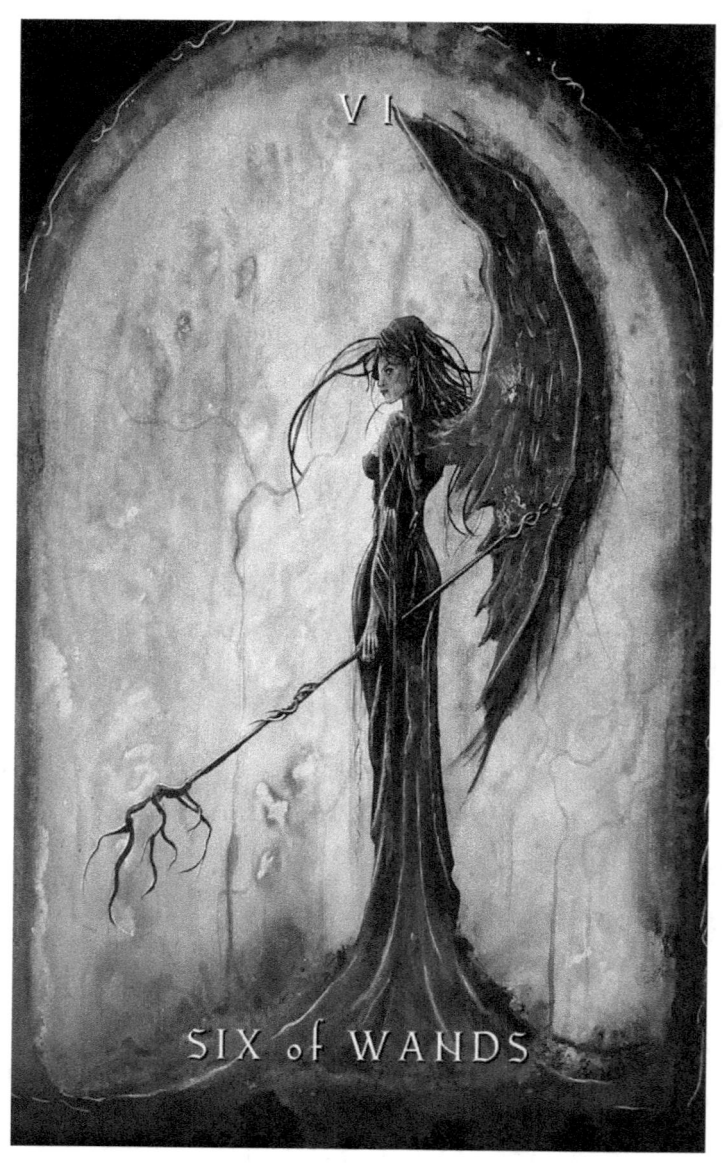

Six of Wands

Accomplishment. Recognition

Perhaps you've achieved something.

A goal reached.

A milestone attained.

A mountain scaled.

The Six of Wands is simple and clear in its message. You've met the challenge of the hour, and you're ready to stand proudly on a field of victory. This is one of those moments no one can take away from you. Whatever it took you to get to this point, honor the experience.

And honor yourself.

This may be but one step of many in the long journey you've prepared for yourself. And yet, for one shining moment, be free to celebrate, no matter whether your victory is vast or diminutive.

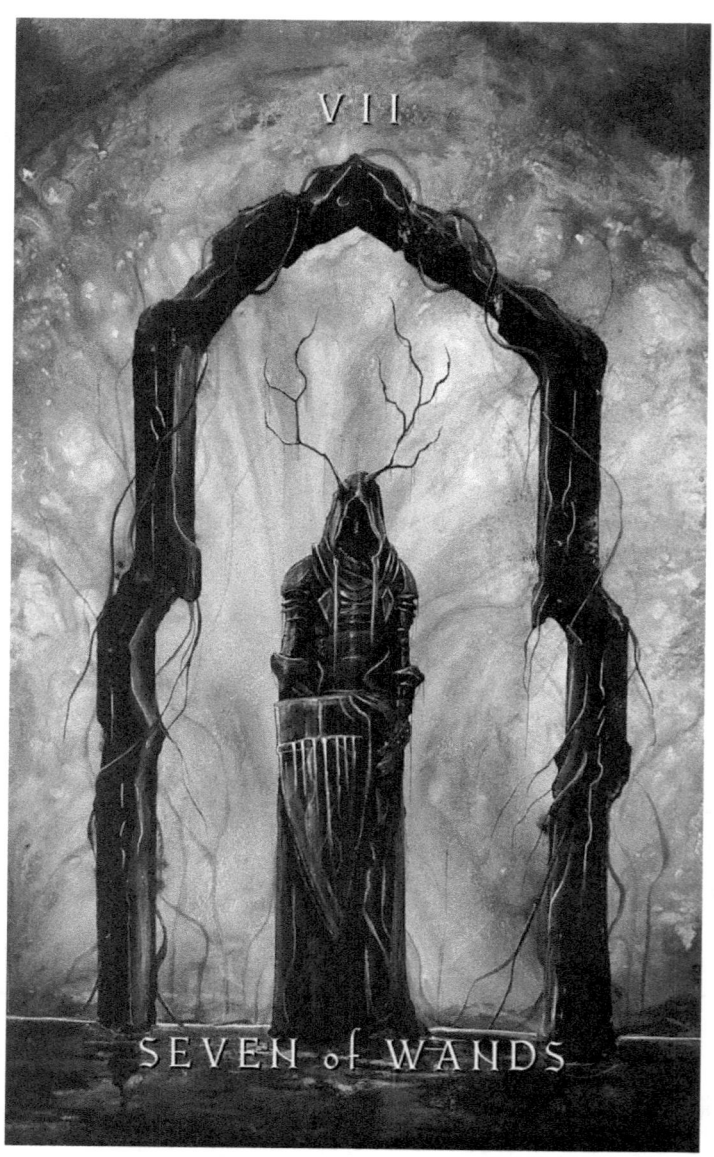

Seven of Wands

None Shall Pass

Victory is far from eternal.

Having earned a position of honor or attained a goal long-desired, you may find yourself needing to defend your newly-gained territory. The Seven of Wands suggests that with even with the smallest successes come new challenges.

And *challengers.*

It's time to stand firm. No one must be allowed to take away what you've earned. Something or someone might approach you with the aim of knocking you down a peg or three.

If you're in a position of leadership, now is the time to demonstrate your skill. If a covetous or even malicious person seeks to take something of yours, you'll need to spare no effort in defending yourself. Use all your resources: your intellect, your intuition, and your personal convictions. Gather friends and supporters close to your side.

Defend yourself at all costs.

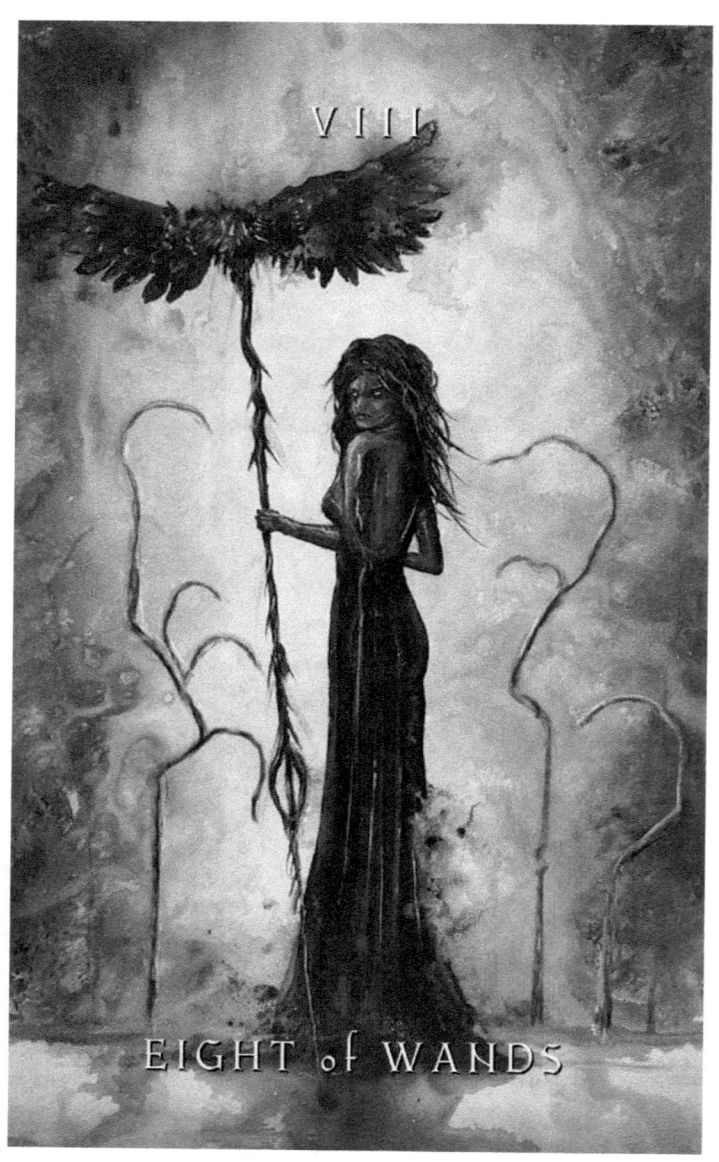

Eight of Wands

Go With the Flow

If we view the suits of the Minor Arcana as smaller journeys through life (compared to the Major Arcana) then perhaps you're able to see a pattern emerging. From the celebratory moments of the Six of Wands to the harsh challenges of the Five and Seven of Wands, you're now on a rising pathway toward the Queen and King cards.

Think of the Eight of Wands as motion incarnate. The river of life flows swiftly around you, and you may find yourself caught in the current.

Fear not. This day is not for drowning.

This is one of those moments during which, if you are focused, determined, and ready to spread your wings, you can make rapid and positive movements toward your desires. In love, in relationships and careers, in spiritual pursuits, if your mind is in the right place, the energy of these next moments can propel you into the future much faster than anticipated.

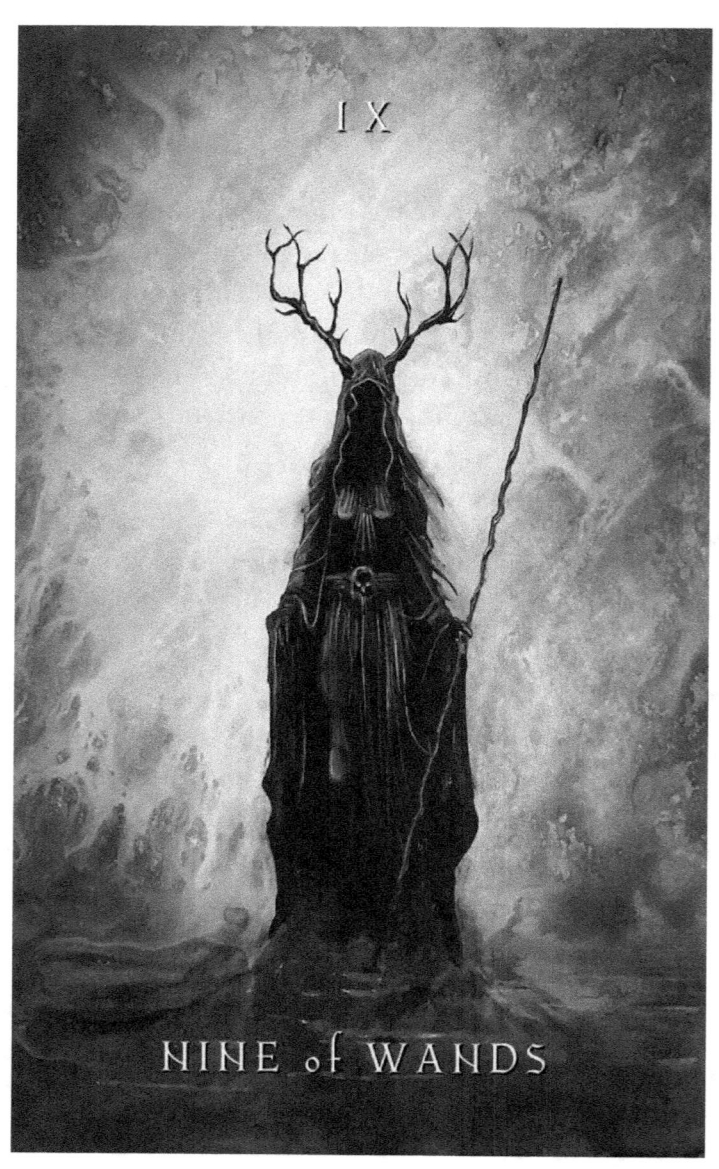

Nine of Wands

Reflection. Resilience

You're weary...so weary. Your journey has been long and difficult. Your deserved reward hasn't yet arrived, and you're wondering when will it *ever*.

Look at yourself in the mirror. Do you see defeat? Are you too tired to press on?

'Never,' you must say.

All your many small successes and setbacks are now behind you, and it's time to show your true mettle. The advice of the Nine of Wands is to glean the good and useful experiences of the past, while shedding all the things that hold you back. From now on, only those things which serve you well should remain with you. Your doubt and disillusionment must be cast aside. Think of yourself not as exhausted, but as battle-tested. The prize can be yours, if only have the nerve to make it so.

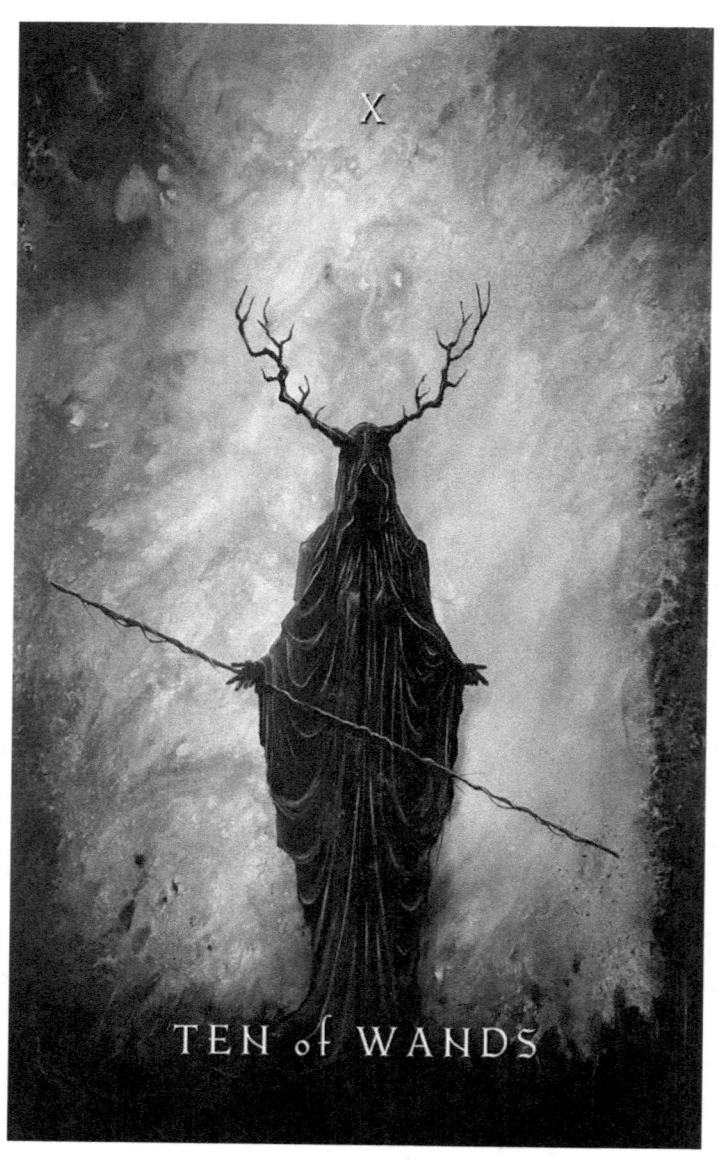

Ten of Wands

The Weight of Expectation

Have you ever reached the end of a long journey, a hard year's work, or a deep spiritual endeavor...
...and found the experience lacking?

Where you expected triumph, perhaps instead you feel *heavy* with the burdens of life?

Where you hoped for rest and relaxation, you find only more work to be done?

The expectations upon you, whether self-imposed or foisted onto your shoulders by others in your life, are too much. The Ten of Wands implores you to halt and take a good long look at your life. These burdens of yours...they needn't be carried alone. It's time to share the load. Release yourself from expectation. Appreciate what you have, even when it doesn't perfectly align with what you hoped.

The word I like to use here is *balance*. We're human, and even the most successful and responsible of us can only carry so much. Consider all the many things you carry, and let go of those things which bring pressure and pain to your life. Only then can you find a pleasant equilibrium.

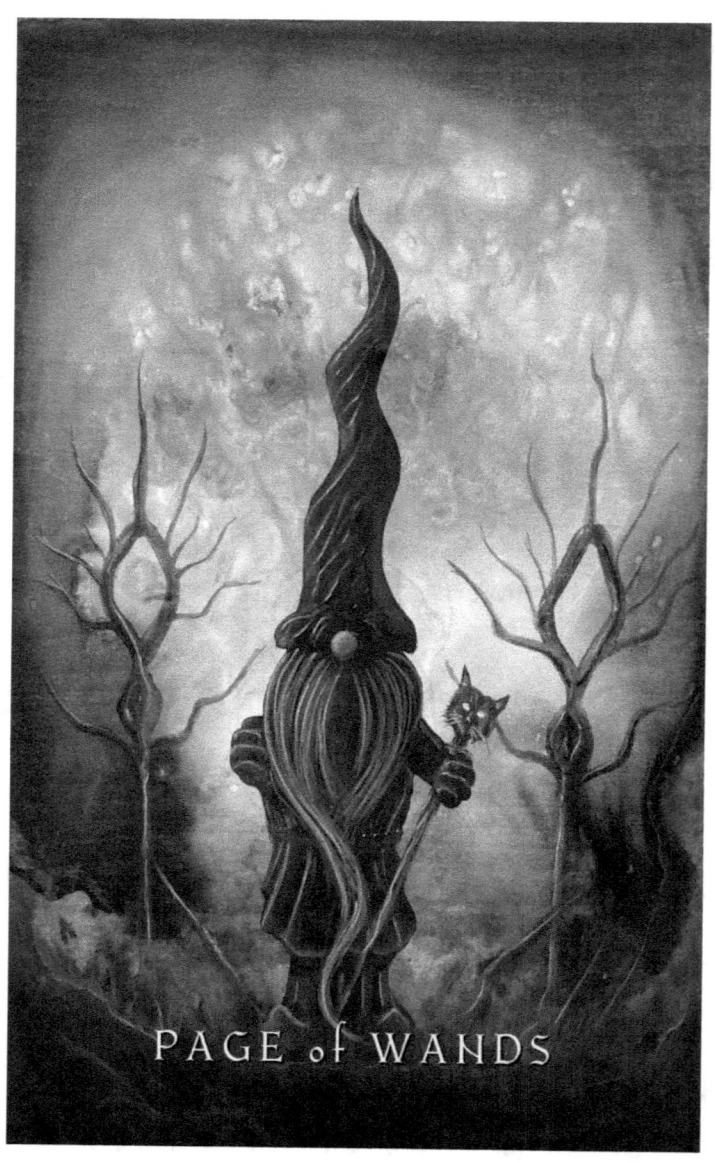

Page of Wands

Embodiment of Enthusiasm

Within each suit, the Pages are somewhat like fresh-eyed versions of The Fool.

They're hopeful. They're free-spirited. They're bursting with life.

Just like you, *right?*

Essentially, the Page of Wands appears when it's time for you to reconnect with the virtues of purity, playfulness, creativity, and childless innocence. Way deep down, the youthful spirit within you wants to erupt into the world.

This energy exists inside you. Now all it needs is focus.

Your homework assignment tonight, after pulling the Page of Wands? Search for the source of your budding inspiration. Find what it is you *really* want to do with this energy. Make an oath to yourself to turn potential into reality.

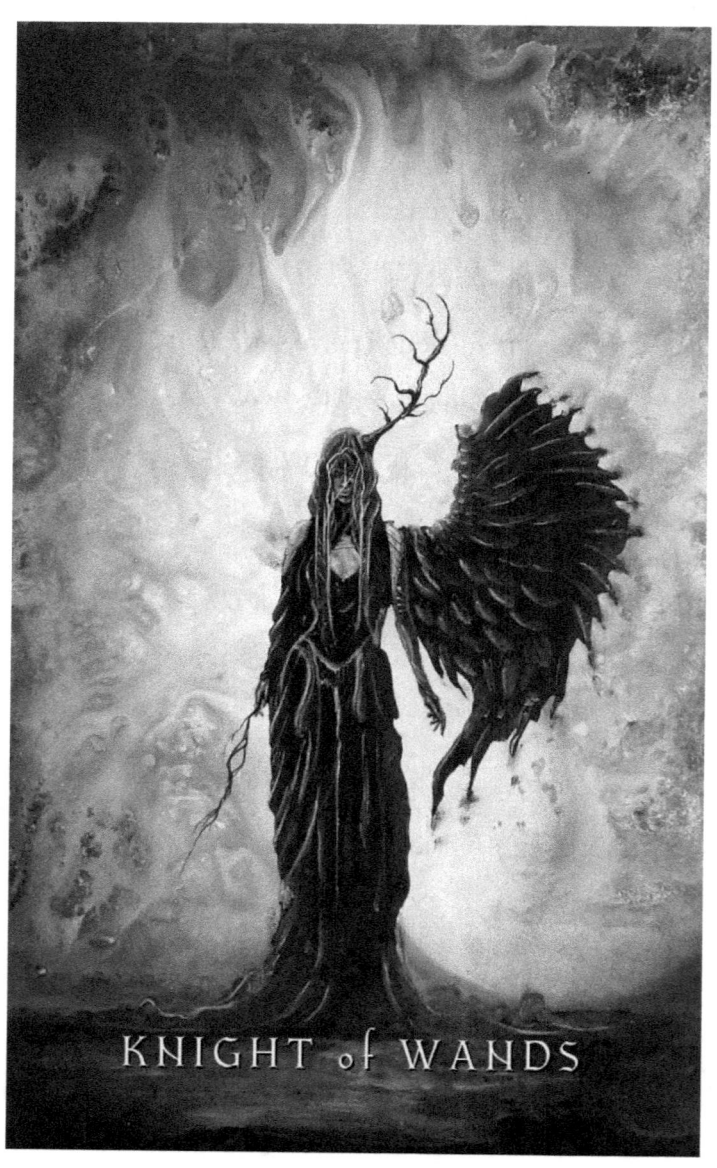

Knight of Wands

Fearless, Impulsive, Visionary

The Page of Wands has grown-up.

Ideas have become action. Potential is now *movement.*

It must be thrilling indeed to shed one's fears and doubts. Dangerous, perhaps. Reckless, for certain. And yet there are times in life during which desire, passion, and adventure must absolutely replace our static routines.

For you, this appears to be one of those times.

Oh, a word to the wise:

If the Knight of Wands describes you, consider taking a moment (just a few short breaths, really) to develop some semblance of a strategy. If you're traveling far from home, determine a route. If you intend to experience something for the very first time, think about how you intend to approach it. Adventure can and will set your heart free, but without forethought, it can end just as quickly as it begins.

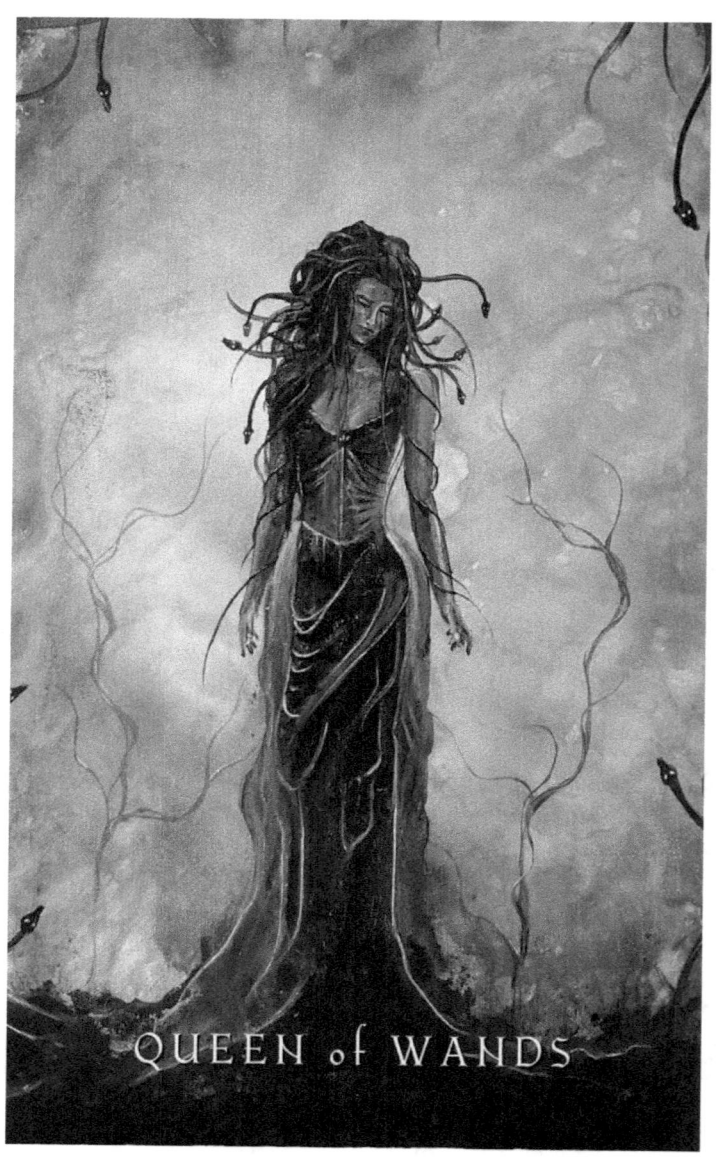

Queen of Wands

Radiance

There is no rest for one who is queen. No matter. She'll thrive nonetheless.

The Queen of Wands suggests vast power within you. Whether you're aware of your shadow-self or not, consider this list of abilities you likely possess:

Charisma. Empathy. Vitality. Creativity.

If you desire it, you can become *unstoppable.*

Encountering the Queen of Wands suggests that you are or are about to become the center of attention. There's something radiant about you right now, an inner light which begs to be expressed openly. If this doesn't feel like you at the moment, these traits might exist in someone close to your heart. A supporter, perhaps. A valuable friend. In any case, consider embracing your most powerful traits. As queen, you're able to draw people to the noblest causes. Great things could result, if only you will take the lead.

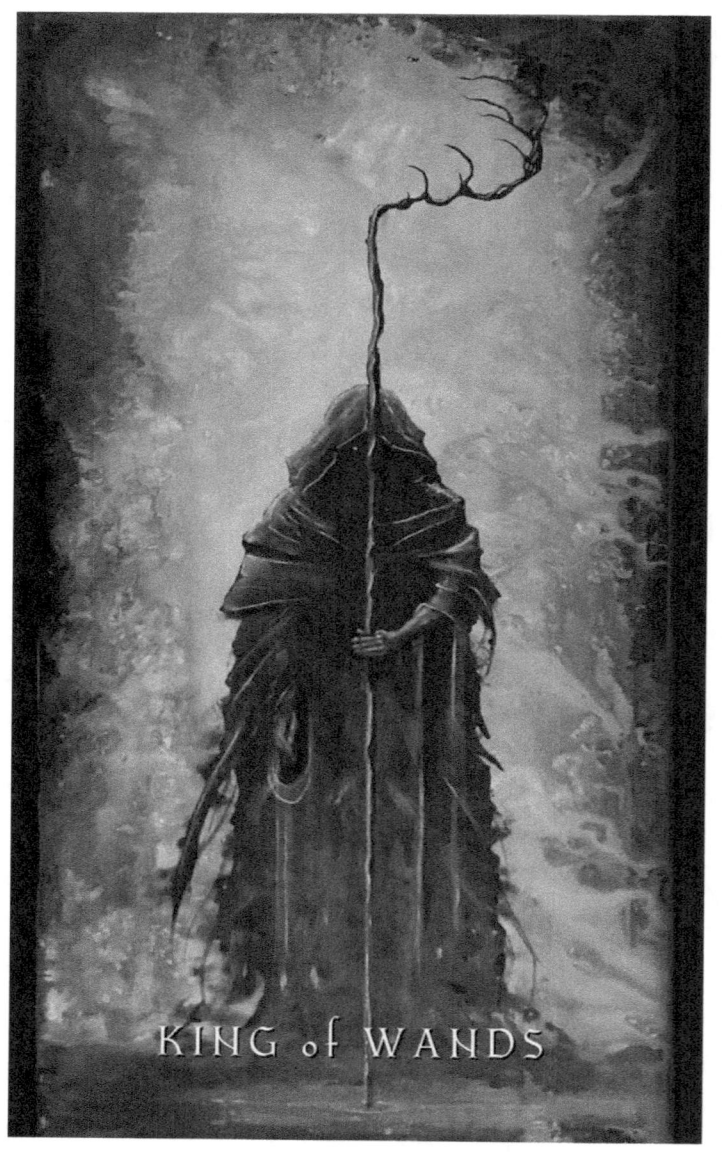

King of Wands

The Visionary

At times, we must follow.

At other, we must *lead.*

There's an opportunity at hand, or so the King of Wands suggests. Even if you don't *feel* like a natural leader at heart, the present moment desires that you share your expertise with the world. You have resources at your disposal, skills that perhaps you haven't yet revealed. And now more than ever, you are needed.

A king must have clarity. If not through raw authority, they must command respect and build relationships with others using an even temper and a sense of justice. Above all, a king must remain composed, even in times of trouble.

We're not talking about some mystical, far-fetched fantasy novel character here. We're talking about *you.* You may soon find yourself in a position of leadership or with a heavy decision to make which affects many others. Meaning, the moment is *now* during which you need to channel your inner monarch. Be fair, be benevolent, be approachable, but also be strong, confident, and commit to taking action with forethought and intent.

Cups

Cups are associated with emotion, relationships, creativity, and deep connection with others. It represents the element of water. Mutable and ever-changing, the energy of Cups is always receptive to change.

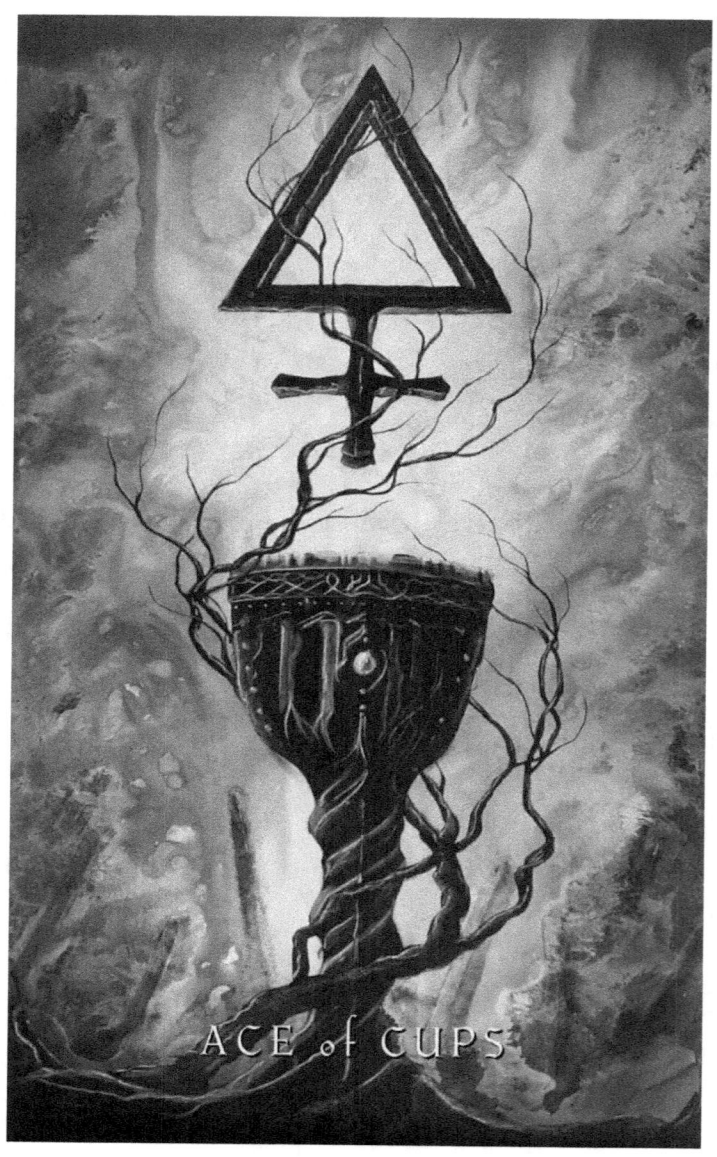

Ace of Cups

Awakening, Renewal

The past can't hurt you.
Yesterday can be overcome.
These are concepts on which I like to focus when considering the Ace of Cups. The idea is that each day is utterly new, and that we are awake in the present moment, far from the dreams of yesteryear.
One (or several) of these is on the horizon:

New love
A fresh and exciting opportunity
A creative idea blossoming
A spiritual awakening

To drink from the Ace of Cups is to move forward with an open heart. As in, *wide*-open. Drop the baggage you usually carry and experience the present moment for what it truly is—
A brand-new day.

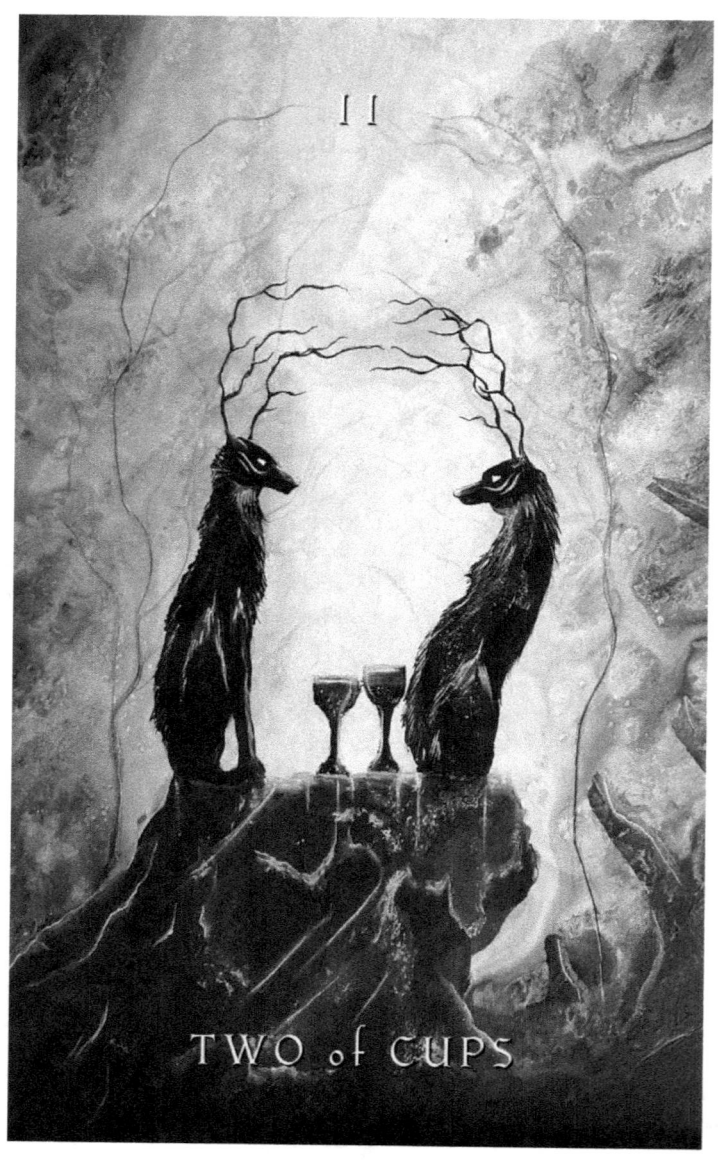

Two of Cups

New Relationship

The Two of Cups – some people's favorite tarot card to pull.

This rather pleasant card portends a new partnership both harmonious and mutually beneficial. It might be a romantic relationship, a new friendship, or a valuable business partnership. What's likely is that you will feel strongly connected to a new person in your life.

Whatever the nature of your relationship with this person, you may find that you're naturally in sync with one another. Like a gift from the universe, the two of you (or more...you never know) will arrive at a warm understanding early and often.

The best relationships (of all kinds) are those in which everyone involved is equally invested. Since we're deep into the suit of Cups, think of it like a single bottle of wine poured evenly between two cups. Keep the flow balanced, and all will be well.

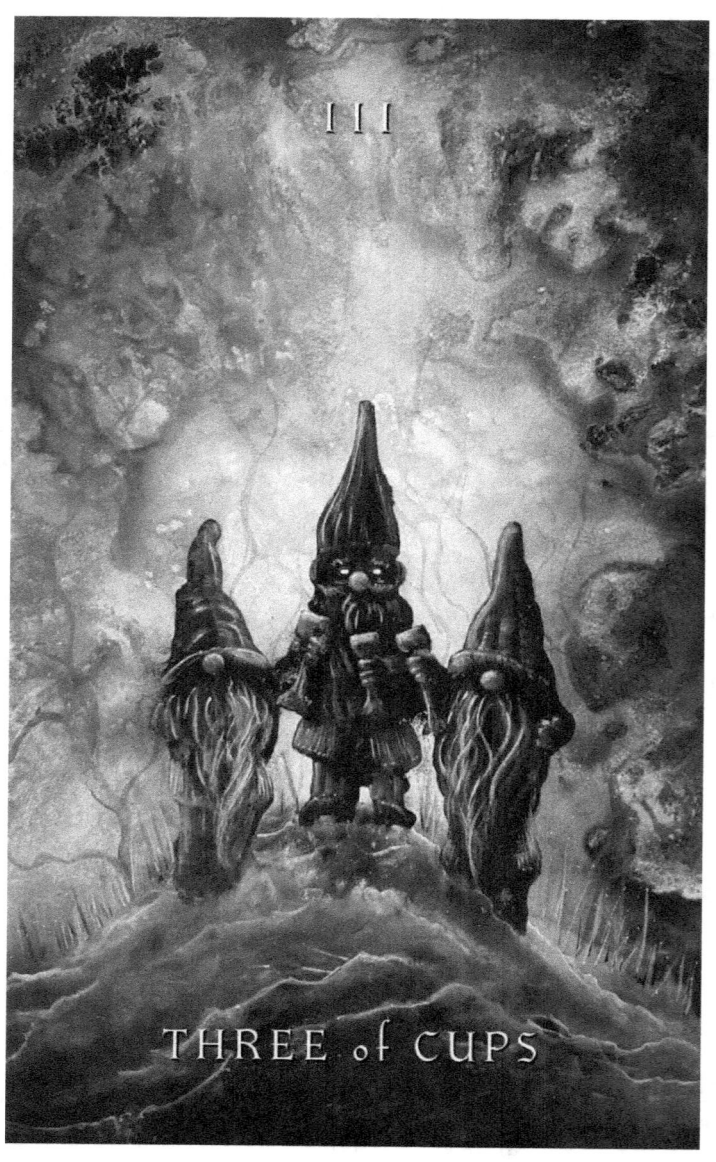

Three of Cups

A Celebratory Moment

Gather your friends close. It's time for a party.

The Three of Cups is a symbol for camaraderie, friendship, fun, and celebrating with those people you hold dearest in life. Lucky you. If you've arrived at this card, the suggestion is that such a moment will arrived either immediately or very soon.

A key takeaway — don't always think of the Three of Cups as a literal party. For you, it could mean a collaboration of kindred spirits, a new project taking flight with your favorite co-creators, or a joining of positive energies toward a mutually-desired goal.

This moment of connection, like any other in life, could be ephemeral. Savor it while it lasts. Soak it up for all it's worth.

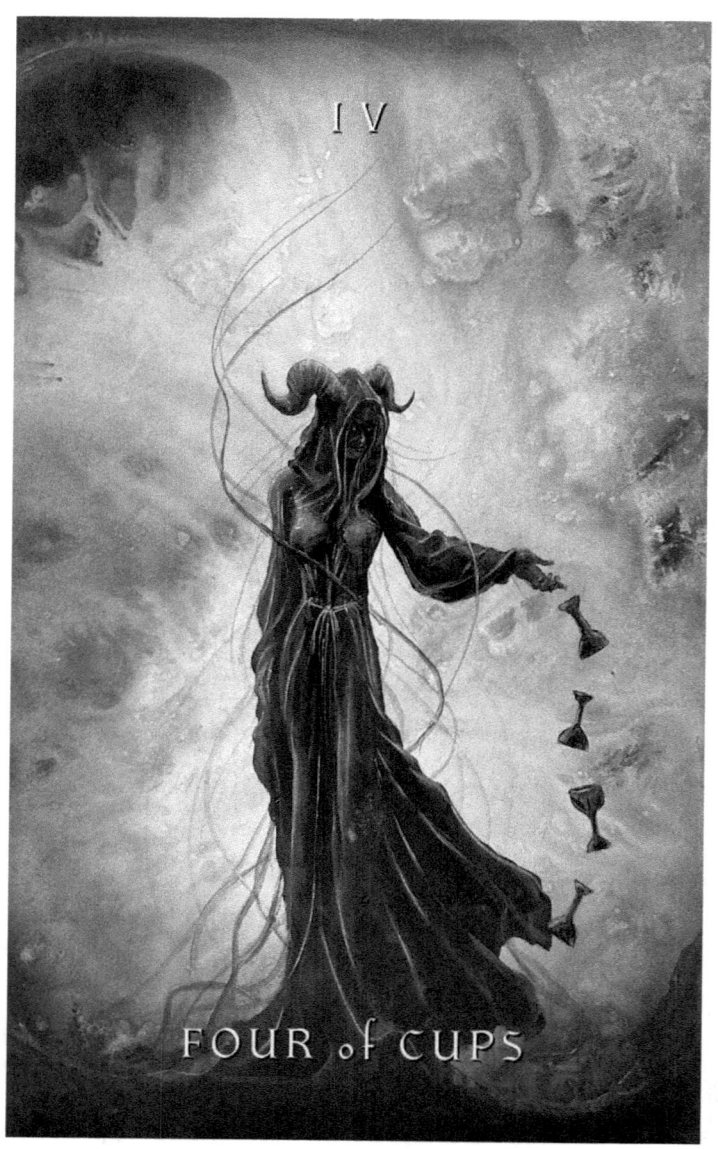

Four of Cups

The Answer is 'No'

Sometimes we reach a point in our lives during which none of the opportunities before us are satisfactory.

Gifts, prospects, potential for change lie within our grasp, yet we're apathetic. We just don't care.

It would be easy to claim this reaction is bad, and should be changed immediately, but it's never quite that simple. The underlying message here is that when the Four of Cups arrives, it's because you're in touch with your internal self, and external influences aren't what you presently need.

In other words, now is *not* the time. Internalizing your thoughts and desires is something we must all do. We need to know that what's being offered is the right fit for us. Specifically, you're in no mood to be pushed, prodded, or manipulated into taking a certain path. You deserve clarity. Contemplate the opportunities within each of the cups offered to you, and drink only from the right one.

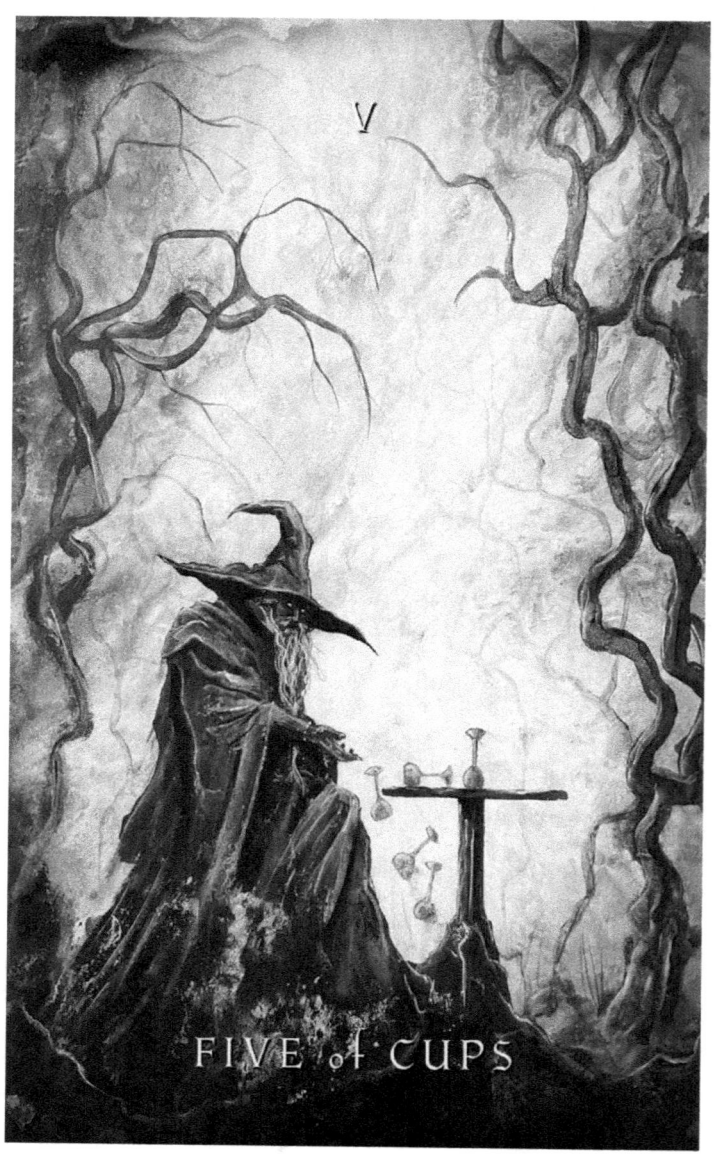

Five of Cups

Letting Go

Most of the anxieties we face in life are the result of past disappointments.

Remember this well.

Disappointment, wallowing, regret – these are the energies of the Five of Cups. As unpleasant as it is, you *can* release these feelings if you're willing to let go. Dwelling in days gone by, reliving difficult moments from the past, and thoughts of "what if?" will keep you from focusing on the here and now.

Don't. Just don't.

Let yesterday die. Sweep away the bitter cups of your previous self. Let tomorrow refill and refuel you.

The challenge of the Five of Cups is to understand that even the worst moments of the past can have a positive impact on your life. If you allow it, the trials of history will make you resilient. Learn the lessons you need, and release everything else.

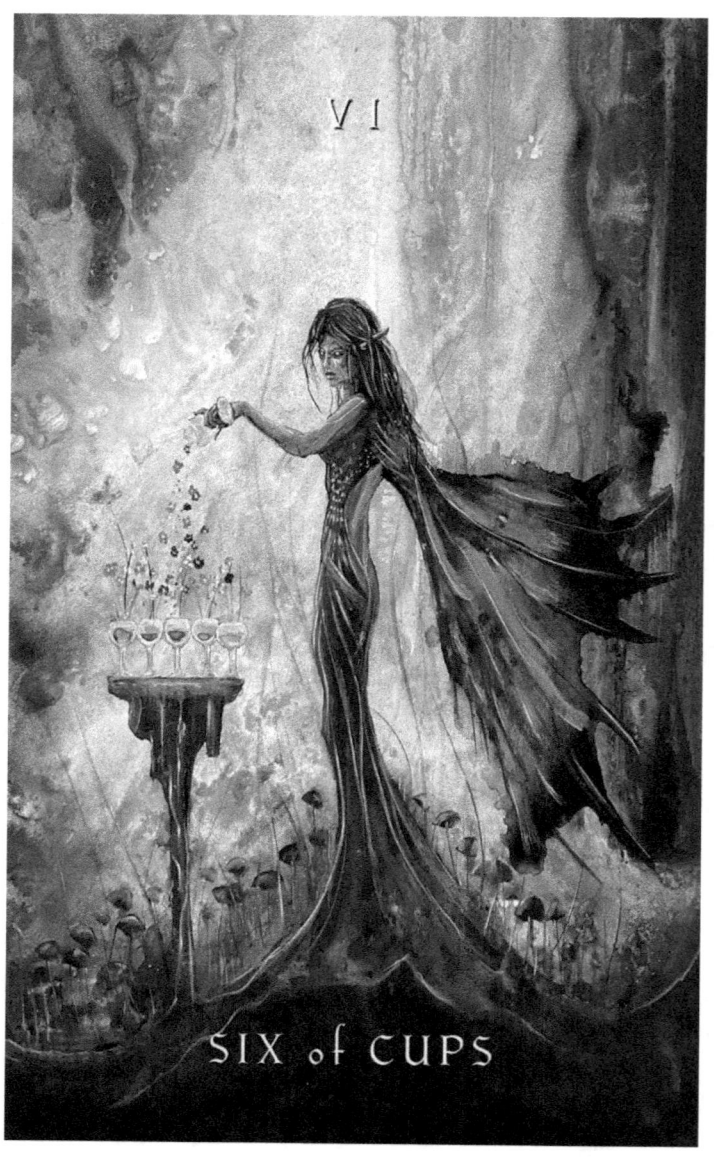

Six of Cups

Reconnecting to Past Joy

Now that we've moved past the unhappy energy of the Five of Cups, let's look at the past in a brighter light.

Close your eyes and think of *home*.

Perhaps it's a place, but just as likely, *home* is a state of mind. It's where you go when you need to convalesce, to let go of all your troubles.

The Six of Cups wants you to remember:

Fond memories from yesteryear

A person you haven't seen in a long time

Something wonderful from your childhood

A place you used to inhabit...and love

And now the Six of Cups wants you to pour the fine wine of those almost-forgotten days into the goblet of your current life. In other words, it's time to reconnect, to remember, and to bring some of the energy from the past into the present. The key here is not to idealize those days, but to take what is good from them and bring yourself peace in the here and now.

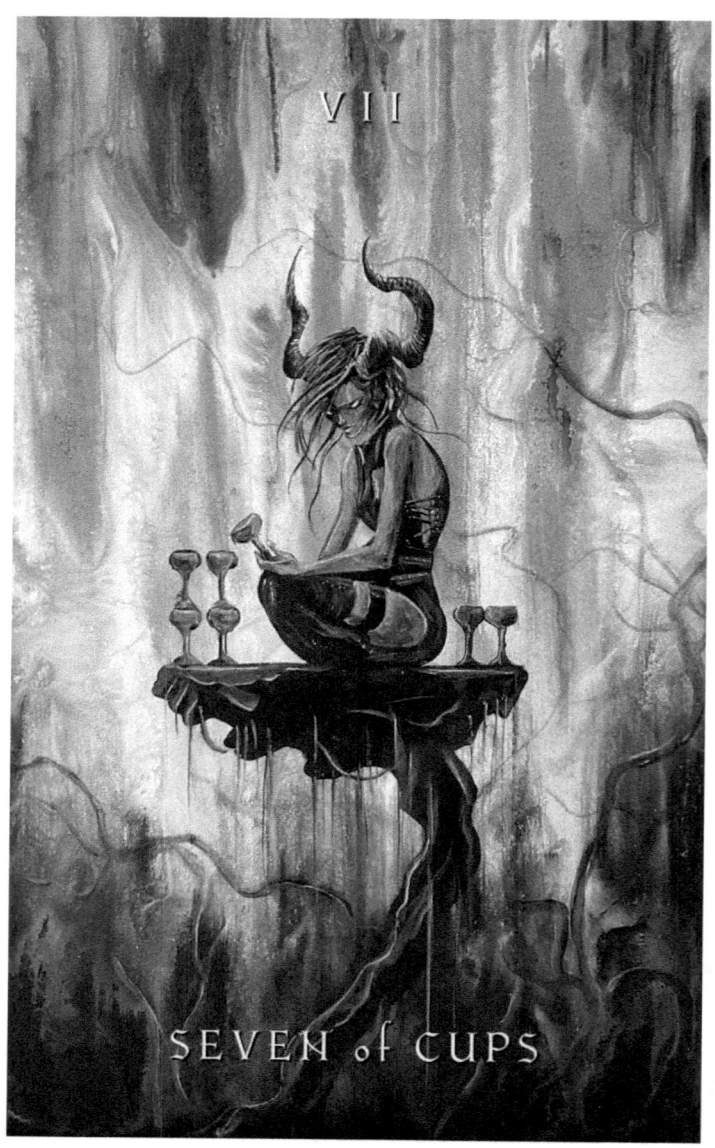

Seven of Cups

Choices, Choices

The Seven of Cups are full to the brim with the energy of choices or opportunities.

So many options. So many paths you could take.

At the crossroads of life, you will find yourself overwhelmed, indecisive, paralyzed. You must determine which of these choices are realistic...

...and which are mere fantasy.

Of all the roads before you, which one is the *least* fantastical, the *most* true to what you want? What effort on your behalf is needed to make your dreams into reality? Very soon, you will require a period of self-reflection to identify which choice is not only right for you, but also the most authentic for you in the here and now.

The challenge of the Seven of Cups is to keep yourself from escaping into fantasy. It may be tempting to stay within the dreamy realm of possibility and not take any steps towards bringing something into fruition. Daydreams, wishful thinking, and fantasies are an important part of manifesting, but the reality is about putting in the hard work to make something happen.

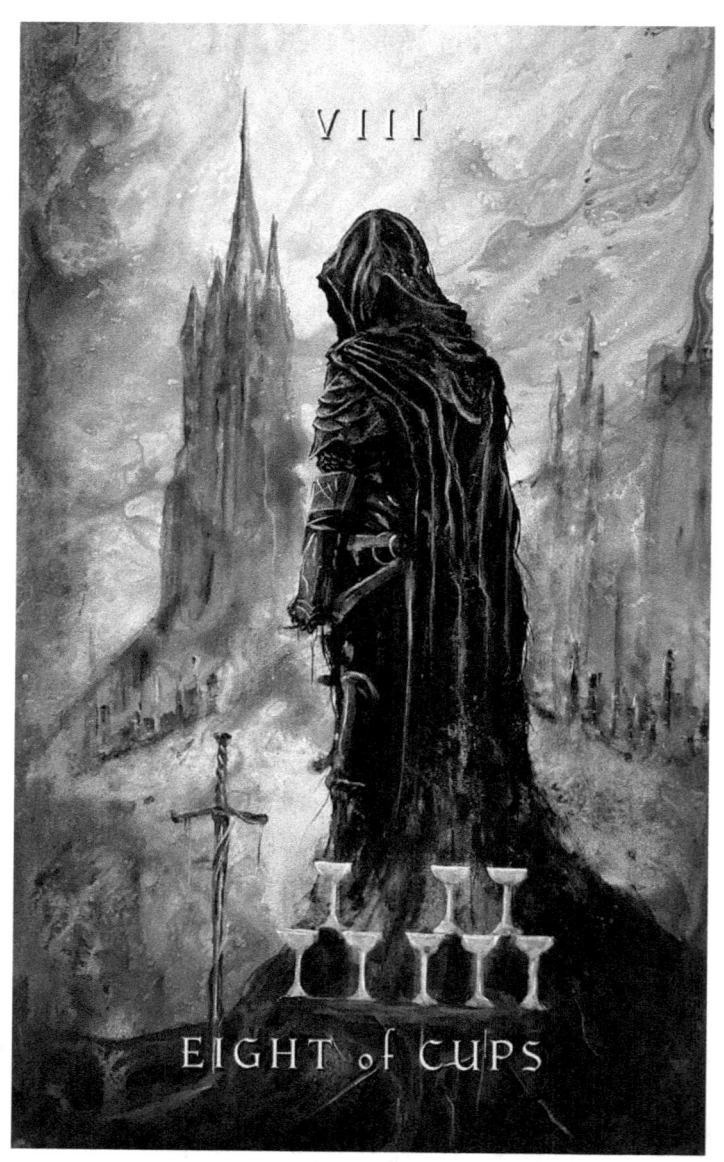

Eight of Cups

Leave it All Behind

Something is missing.

Something hasn't turned out the way you hoped.

And now it seems your only recourse is to walk away.

The Eight of Cups suggests deep unfulfillment. Perhaps you were led to believe your cups would be full of wine (and riches) but the reality is they were empty all along. This is less likely to represent actual material things which are lacking, and more likely to mean a spiritual or emotional absence.

You're thinking, 'Fine. I'll just walk away, and everything will be better." But before you do, it would be wise to pause and contemplate what it is you *really* want. True, the promised cups were empty, but what *do* you desire? Only by getting in touch with your innermost needs can you manifest them being met. If you wander away from one place of shadow into another, the cycle of disappointment will continue.

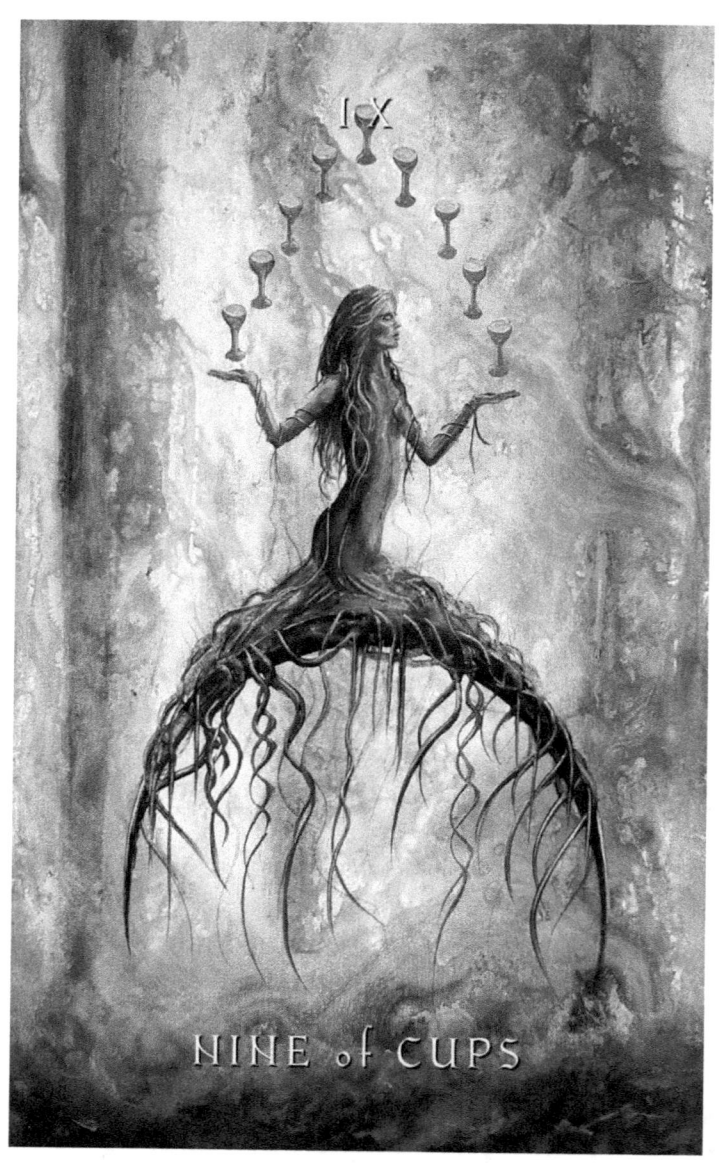

Nine of Cups

Fulfillment

Is this one of the best possible tarot cards to pluck from your deck?

...perhaps.

Tonight, consider holding your cups high, for on this eve they are full of wishes come true. The suggestion of the Nine of Cups is that something deeply personal to you has reached its fruition. In love, in friendship, in either material or emotional realms, something you've wished for has (or is about to) become a reality. The darker aspects of your journey are about to fall away, leaving only the glimmer of success. This is a good day. Cherish it always.

If by some obscure chance you're not feeling the shine of success, it may be that you feel something is missing from the experience. A hollow feeling is possible if you've wished for something that was never in your best interest. If this is the case, it may be the time for some serious soul-searching.

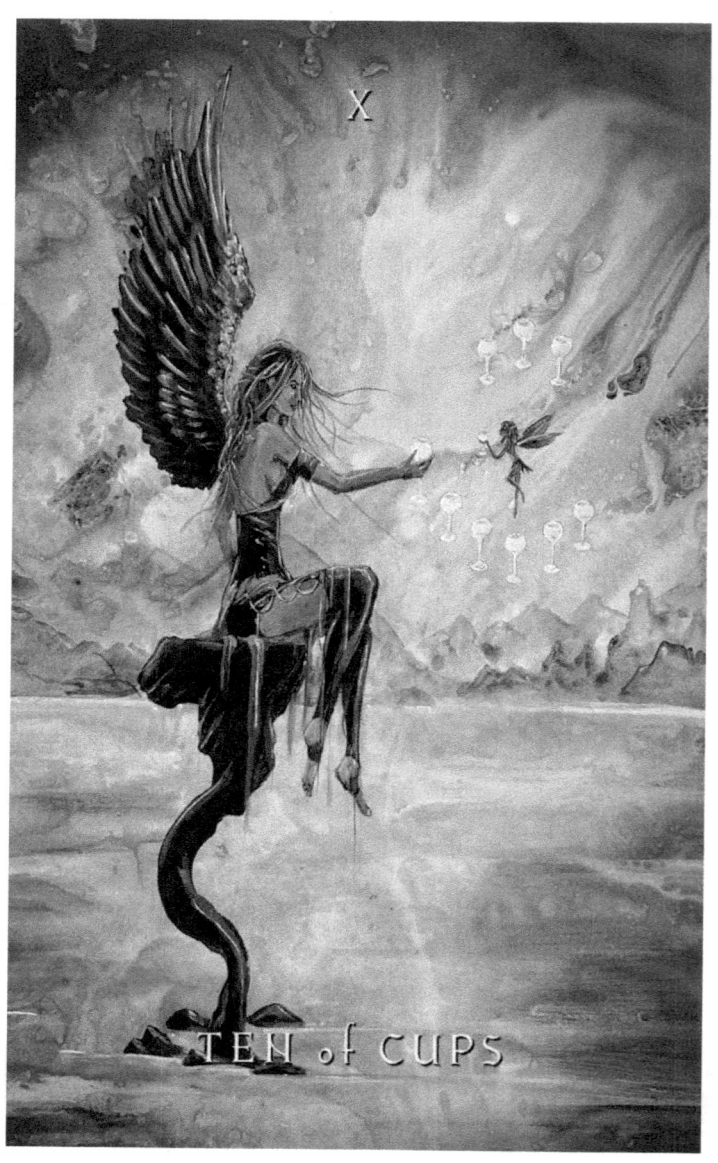

Ten of Cups

Contented Relationships

Let us go a step further than the Nine of Cups is willing to take us. Imagine all the harmony and joy of a deeply personal success, and then spread it across all those you love.

Think of the Ten of Cups as a card of utmost completion, the sort of happiness which simply must be shared with others. Your family, your friends, your lover...they're all within the joyous bounds of harmony and abundance.

The hope here is that you feel a sense of wholeness, completion, and alignment in all of your relationships. The Ten of Cups usually arrives when the positivity of one person's bliss is so effervescent that it spreads to others, casting a net of joy across whole families or groups of friends. Your private wishes for peace, harmony and love are destined to come true, but not merely for yourself.

They're here for *everyone.*

Now is the time to allow yourself to feel good. If your intuition urges you toward a happiness, embrace it.

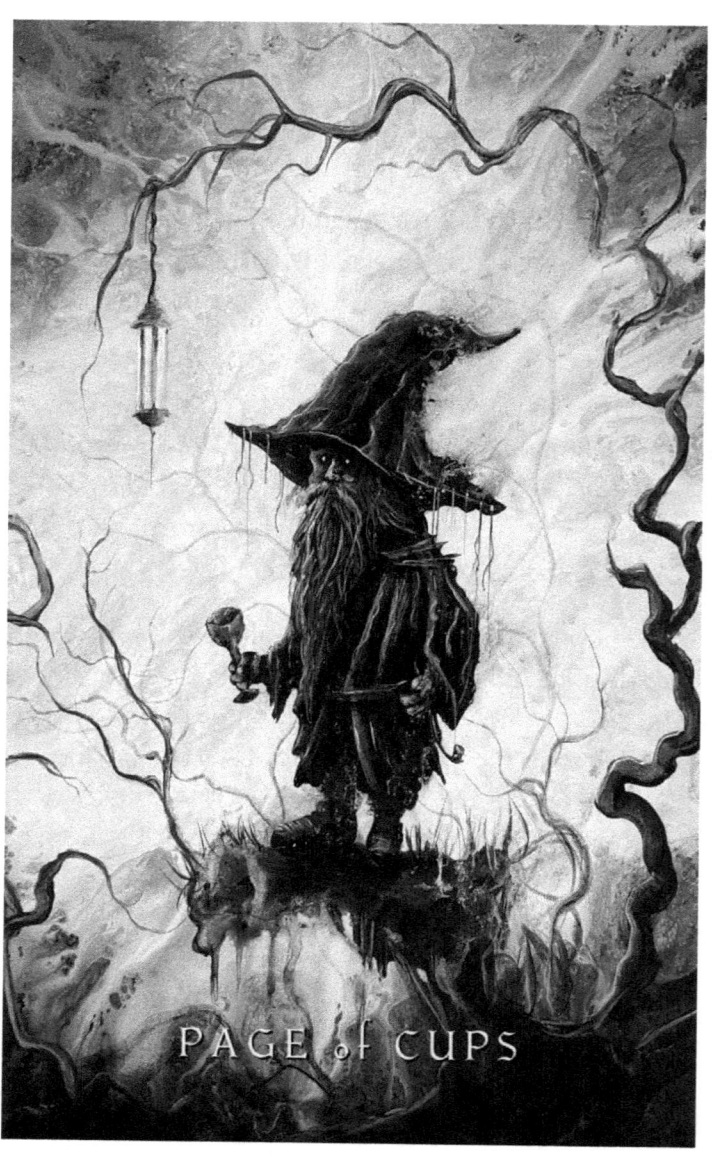

Page of Cups

Bursting with Creativity

You might not believe yourself to be a creative type. Until now, you may have been sleepwalking, awaiting the right spiritual moment to apply what has always existed within you.

But...

The time is now to wear your creative hat.

The Page of Cups, curious and artistic, requests your attention. Even if only on the periphery of your awareness, an opportunity for creation has arisen. This doesn't merely suggest making actual art. The implication is that you are due for a spiritual awakening, a romantic blossoming, or an endeavor of the heart.

Listen closely. The Page of Cups often speaks in whispers, dreams, and daytime reverie. This is your innermost voice speaking. It hates that you've been sleepwalking when you should be creating new things and enjoying new experiences. For the moment, push aside all the distractions and tap into what awaits inside you.

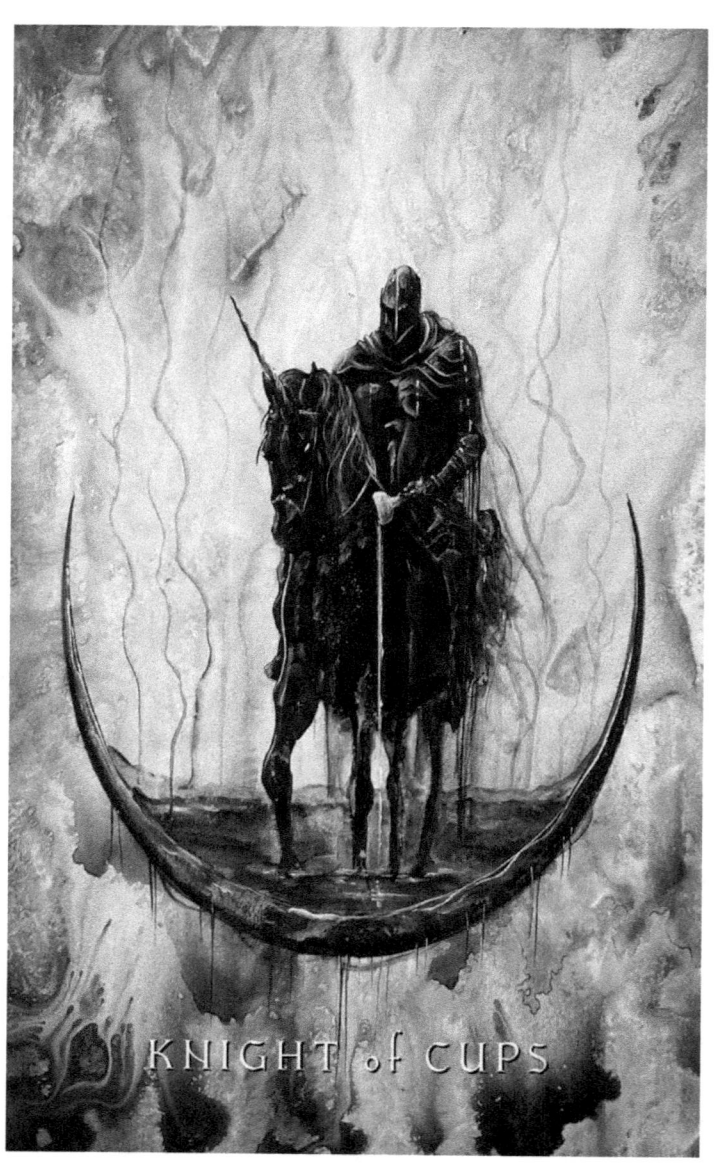

Knight of Cups

The Charmer

If the image of a classic romantic is what you seek, look no further.

The Knight of Cups – a poet, a creative powerhouse, and a lover. He's intuitive, compassionate, and emotional, and not at all afraid to express himself.

Hint: you can be likewise.

In this moment, seat yourself onto the Knight of Cup's stallion. The suggestion here is that you have an opportunity (let's call it an adventure) awaiting you. Perhaps you've been recently inspired, but have yet to take action. Something calls to your heart, needing only for you to set aside your fears and ride directly after it.

You can be a dream-chaser.

You can allow yourself to feel every emotion, no matter how loudly.

You can pursue a new romance, take up a creative pursuit, or fearlessly get in touch with your deepest spiritual cravings.

You are the Knight of Cups.

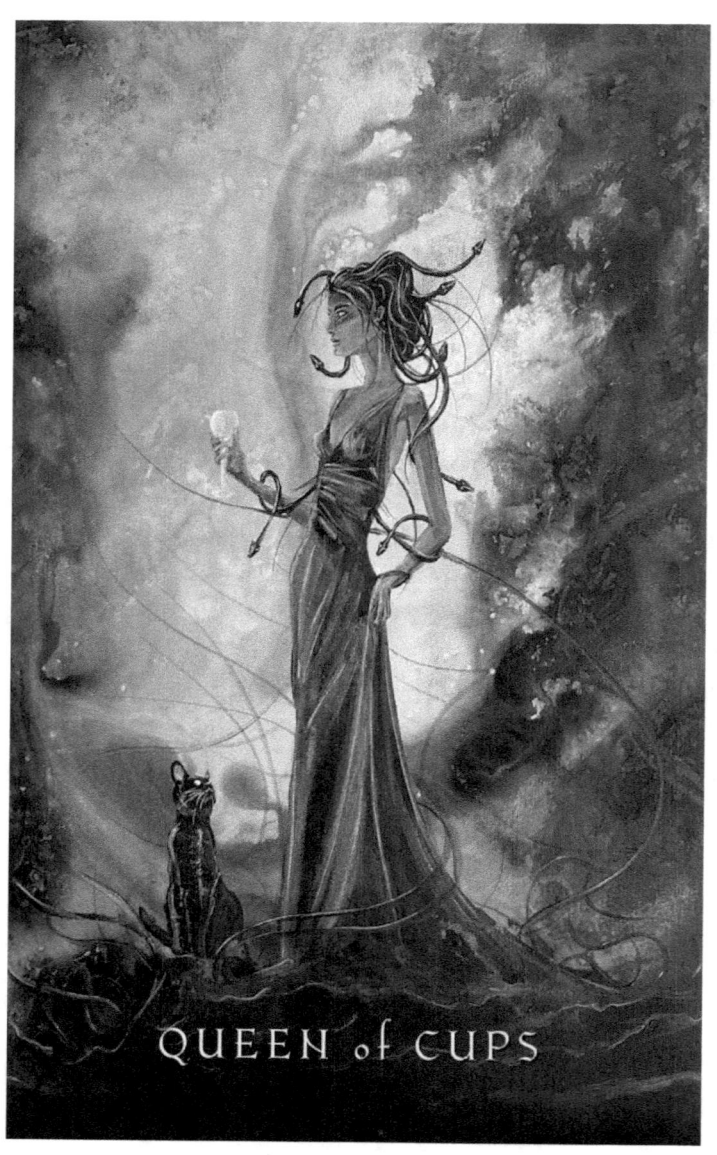

Queen of Cups

Introspective & Nurturing

Lead not with your head.

Lead instead with your *heart.*

Or at least, this is the desire of the Queen of Cups.

Now and then, the time arises when we must shed the tendency to think our way through a situation, and instead *feel* our way. The energy around us is sometimes nebulous, invisible to thought, yet utterly transparent to empathy and intuition.

Look into the mirror. Is this you right now?

The suggestion of the Queen of Cups is that you are to become a nurturer, a confidant, an intuitive guide either to yourself or to some key person in your orbit of loved ones. While the Queen possesses 'mother' energy, it's not always necessary for you to be a mom, but only to behave with the loving patience of one.

Or, rather than nurturing an individual, you may find yourself cradling a new project or endeavor close to your heart. It's important, this thing you're doing, and this is the right time to follow your heart and pour all of your emotion into making it happen.

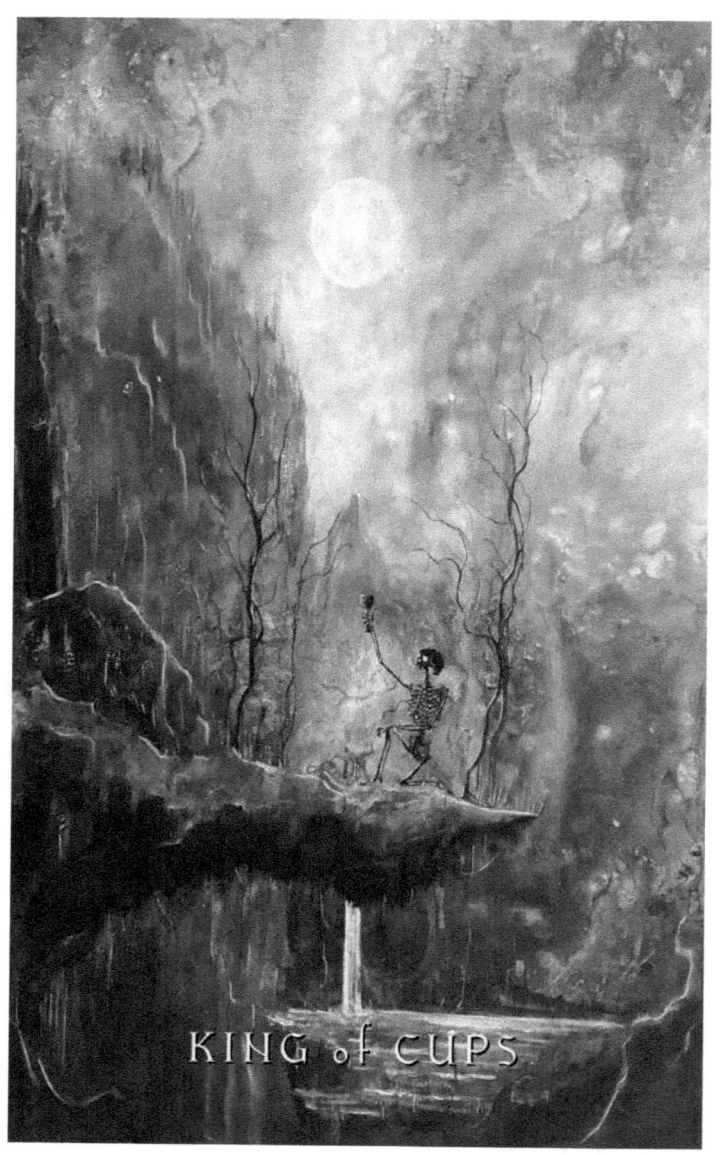

King of Cups

Mediator of Hearts & Minds

Well...are you ready?

This army won't lead itself.

Even outside the realm of tarot, we could all benefit from the King of Cups' balanced view. He's both rational and intuitive, a thinker *and* a feeler. With a deep understanding of his own nature, he is the ideal problem-solver and decision-maker.

The suggestion when he appears in your card spread is that it's time for you to assume his qualities.

Some things to remember if and when you are called upon to lead or become a guide through a challenging situation:

Seek to be a leader with love and compassion in your heart, and never with a desire for power.

Hear the voices of those who need your strength, and attempt no manipulation or betrayal of their trust.

Above all, be authentic and fair.

Swords

Swords, perhaps the most fearsome of suits, is all about the human intellect. Thoughts, attitudes, long-held beliefs...these are Swords' cutting edge. The element of air is powerful, yet ephemeral, and is ever on the move. Be wary. Be wise.

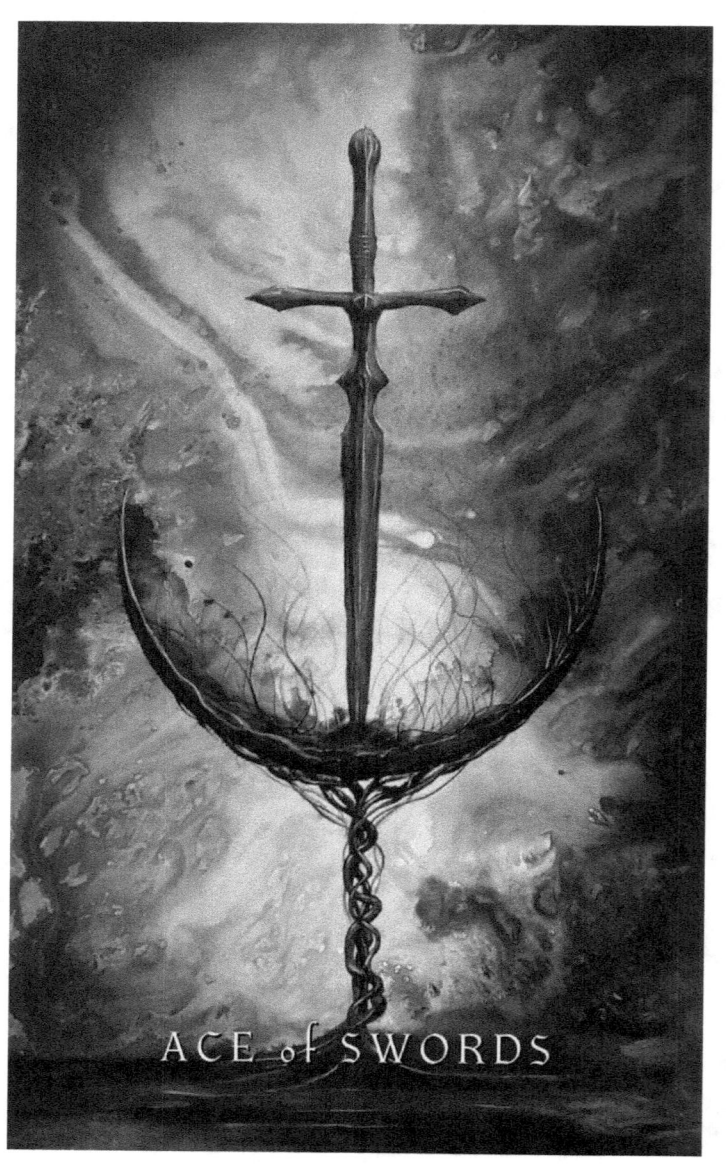

Ace of Swords

Breaking Through

Think of the Ace of Swords as the cutting edge of a new idea.
It's sharp, fresh out of the forge, and ready to be used.

Perhaps your mind is at its most agile right now. You're awake, aware, and focused. This moment, more than any other, is right to carve away all the mental clutter distracting you from what you desire. Wielded with care, you can trim off the useless detritus and render yourself ready to act upon your new and exciting idea.

In these moments, you'll be hard to deceive. You have a sharper perspective on life, and see with great clarity to the horizon of all things which lie before you. Use this time wisely. It's not promised to last forever.

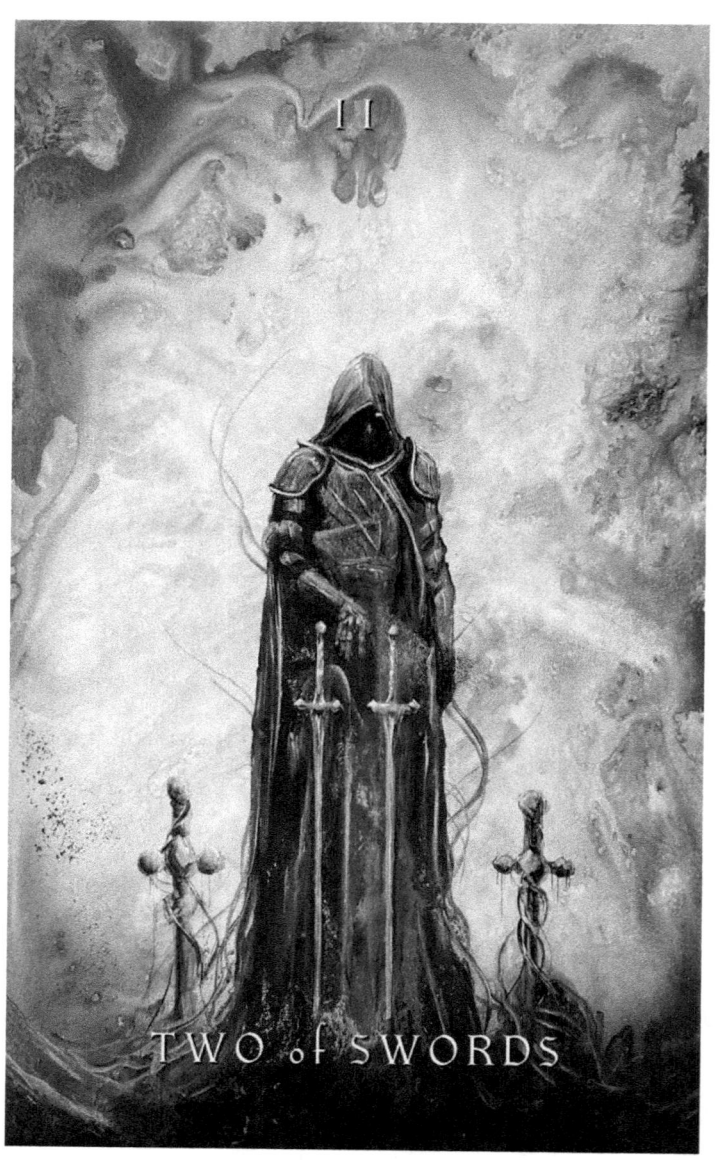

Two of Swords

Choices, Choices

And now it begins, the first of many difficult, double-edged Swords cards.

This is one of those moments during which you're not allowed to sit on the sidelines. Neutrality isn't an option. You won't be able to please everyone...or perhaps *anyone*.

A choice lies ahead. Two forces lie in opposition to one another, vying for your attention. In all likelihood, making this choice will hurt. Something might be gained, but something else could be lost.

One key thing to remember in this moment is that you are not powerless. Before making your choice, you should search for the truth of the matter before you. Seek not to merely pick the lesser of two evils, but instead look for the greater of two goods. Use your mind and skills of deductive reasoning as swords in and of themselves, and wield them with the aim of choosing what is best for everyone, not only yourself.

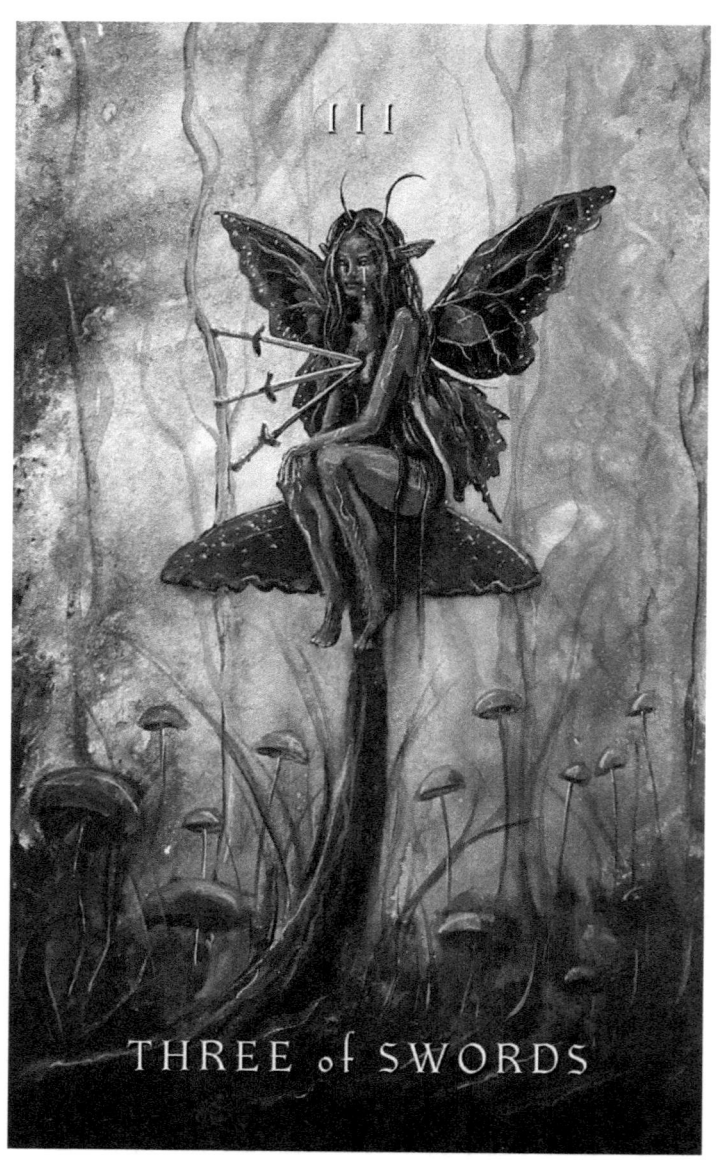

Three of Swords

Shattered Heart

There is no easy way to say this...

Heartbreak and suffering are a natural part of the human experience.

Yes, it will hurt. The three blades of a broken heart, of betrayal's sting, and of deep sorrow are emotions we *all* must experience. For you, in this moment, one of two things might be taking place:

You are experiencing (or about to experience) heartbreak.

You're suffering from something which has already occurred, and it feels dreadfully unshakeable.

What's best for you now is to consider *release*. Try not to look at grief as something which is overcome and cast aside, but as something which becomes a part of us, and not forever in a negative way. Allowing yourself to feel wholly the pain of loss is important, but so too is the healing which comes afterward.

Often, it is our losses in life which become our greatest teachers. We value what we have all the more, and we become stronger and more resilient when the sadness finally wanes.

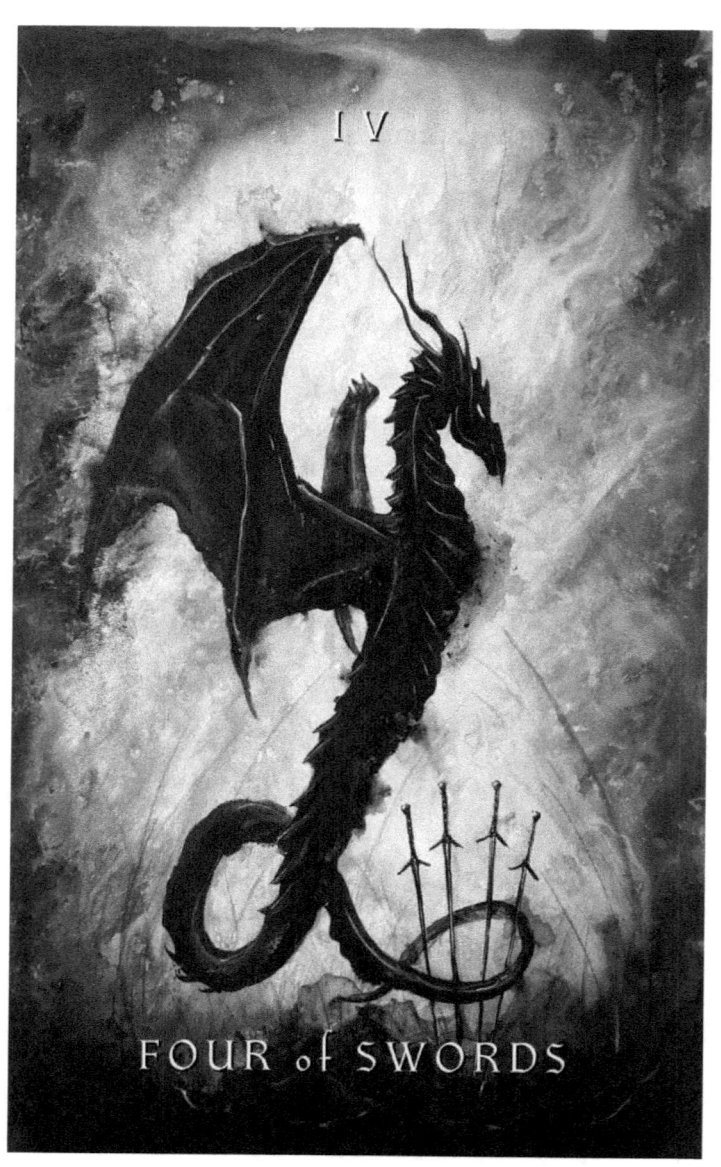

Four of Swords

Retreat

For the moment, the tumultuous energy of Swords is contained.

You need this. Trust me.

In the coming period of time, you'll likely spot a window of opportunity to rest and recuperate. Your temptation might be to keep pushing, to deflect every incoming blow with pure spiritual strength.

Don't.

For now, withdraw from your battles. Escape any and all negative circumstances, and avoid people who exert bad energy in your presence. The time will come when you'll return to the fight, but first you must heal. To be at your full and true self, first you must recharge – body, mind, and soul.

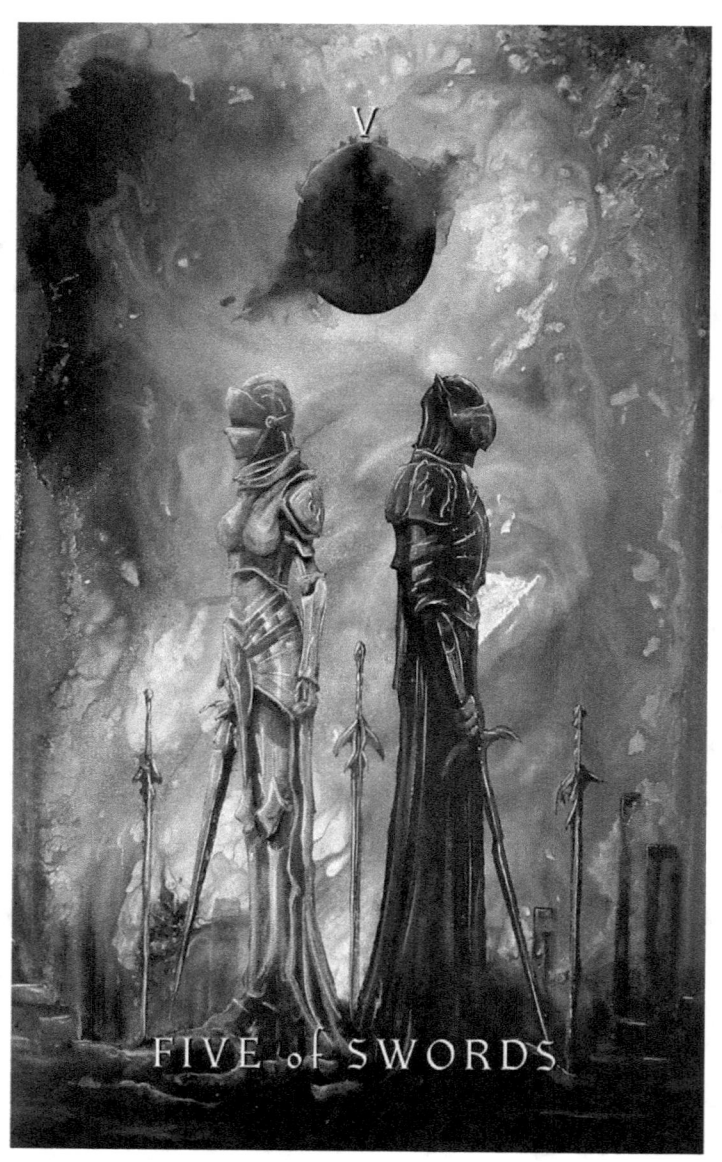

Five of Swords

The Conflict

You've rested and recovered.

And now the battle begins anew.

The Five of Swords is a relentless reminder of some sort of adversity in your life. You're at odds with someone or something, and the nature of this conflict is such that even if you should prevail, the taste of your victory will almost certainly be bittersweet.

There is one path to victory here. Interestingly, it's *not* through winning. Consider the root cause of your conflict. Also consider your adversary, if one exists. Why indeed are you in opposition? What ambitions do you have? What do you really hope to gain through continued conflict? If the cost of winning is too high or the reward too little, you always retain the right to step aside and allow the conflict to wither.

If not, and if you find you must persist, be aware that in some battles (most of them, in fact) there are no victors.

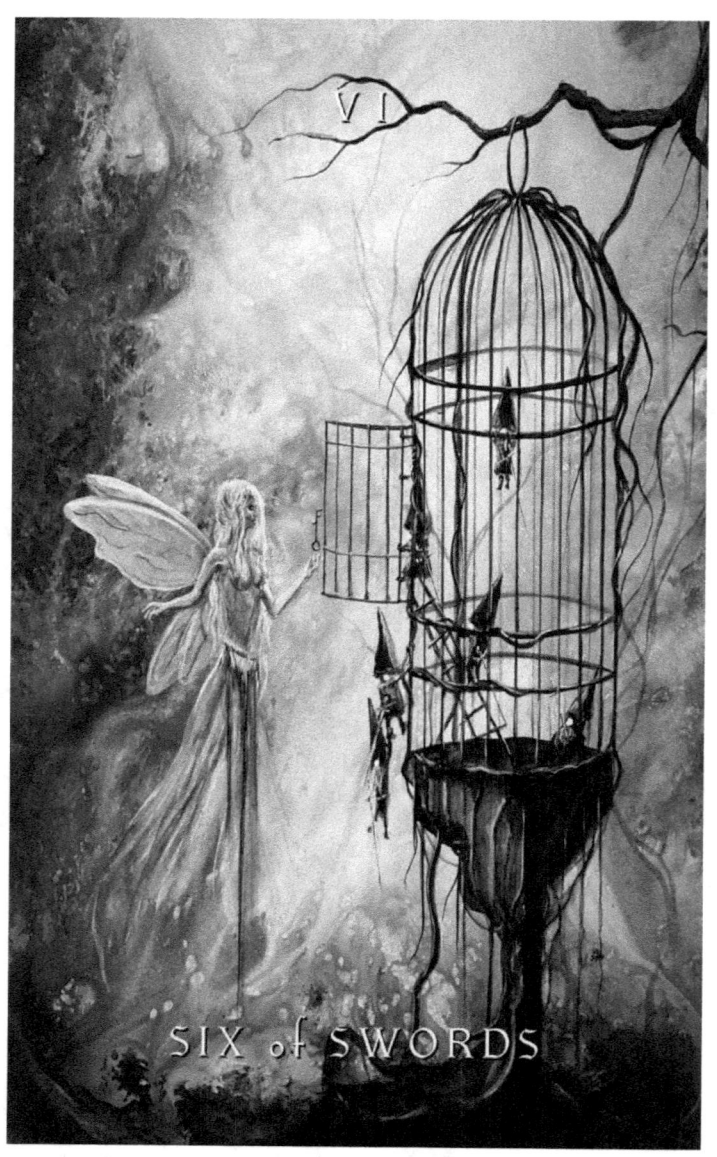

Six of Swords

Liberation

I look at the Six of Swords as a two-fold possibility:

The first – in a very literal and physical sense, is that you are leaving something behind. A job, a home, a person. In most cases (this is the suit of Swords, after all) you don't want to leave this thing behind. You're attached. You desire to stay. You're afraid of the pain of losing something you've long cherished.

The second – in an emotional or spiritual sense, you are walking away from some part of yourself. A behavior you've always had, possibly a coping mechanism or a comforting ritual, is coming to an (possibly sudden) end. And again, it injures you to think of losing it.

In all likelihood, you desire to resist these changes. Giving up a deep comfort, a cherished thing, or a favorite habit of yesteryear is no easy task. And yet, you *need* to let go. You probably can't yet see it, but something beneficial awaits you on the other side.

Again, this is no time to clash swords with yourself. Release yourself from what has served its useful purpose, but is now antiquated. It's the only path to a better tomorrow.

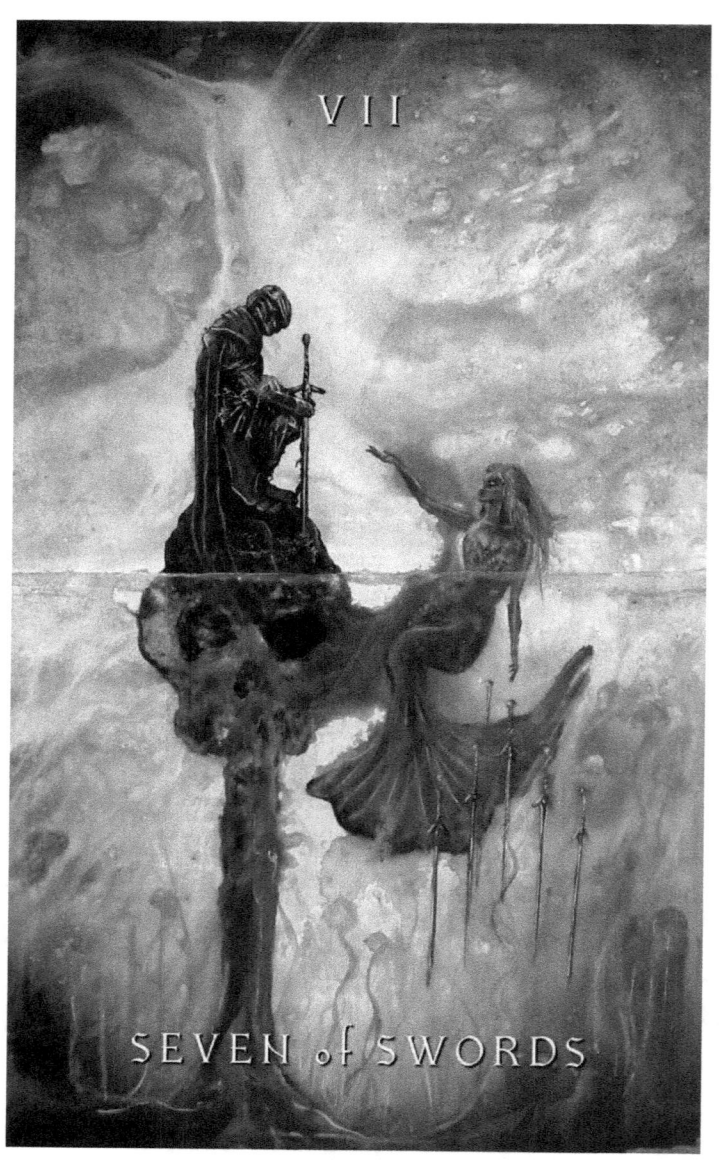

Seven of Swords

Deception & Betrayal

Please, suit of Swords...will you ever relent?

The Seven of Swords suggests that someone in your life is considering deception. Step lightly through the next few days and weeks. Be careful with those in whom you confide or trust with sensitive information. Have eyes in the back of your head, or suffer unseen blades in your back.

Also, look inward. *You* may be the one who is trying to get away with something in the shadows. Perhaps a secret you've been keeping is in danger of being exposed. If this is the case, you'll know it. It's never too late to change direction.

Moreover, The Seven of Swords can arrive up when someone is surreptitiously making their escape. It might be someone trying to leave your life, or it could be *you* seeking to remove yourself from a situation, preferably without others noticing.

The Seven of Swords challenges you to search for the truth, whether it be a situation with someone else or a truth you're hiding within yourself. Be vigilant, my friend. Always.

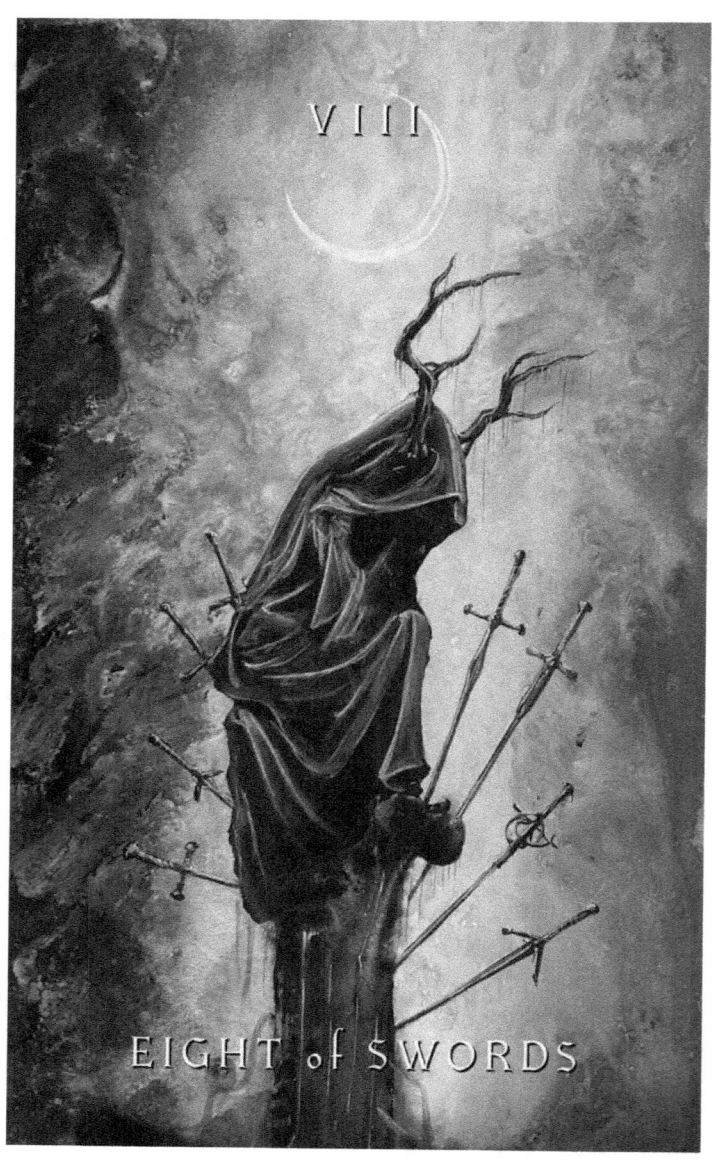

Eight of Swords

Helplessness

The one person holding you back the most in this life?

You.

The suggestion of the Eight of Swords is that, in this current dark moment, you're feeling quite powerless. Whether in your private headspace or in a very real and physical sense, you perceive yourself as being trapped, possibly isolated, and most certainly stuck in place.

Head down, swords surrounding you, you just can't escape.

Or can you?

The reality is, unless you're performing this tarot spread in a literal prison cell, you are not as powerless as you think. Those swords laid all around you? *You* put them there.

The term we need to use here is *self-limiting*. Of course, there are external agents who can cause the perception of being helpless to fall over your eyes, but always you have the power to remove your blindfold, to swat aside the swords, and be free again.

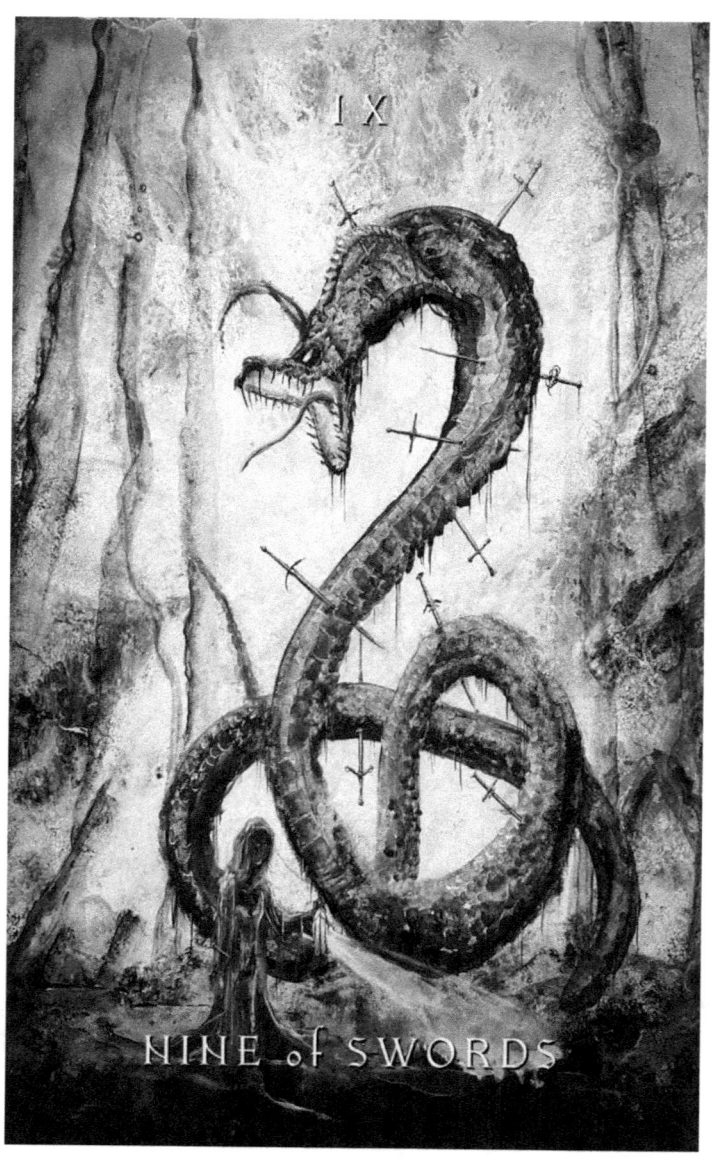

Nine of Swords

Dark Thoughts

Before reading this, go back and read the Eight of Swords definition. The Nine of Swords is what could become of you if you fail to escape the shadow of perceived powerlessness. There. You've been warned.

The Nine of Swords suggests that:

Nightmares, real and imagined, are burdening you.

Anxiety has settled into your bones.

You sense yourself falling into a shadowy mental place from which you doubt you can ever return.

The Nine of Swords is an overthinker's nightmare. It's what becomes of us when we continuously cycle through negative emotions in our heads. It's what happens when we isolate ourselves, offering no respite from fear and doubt.

First and foremost, you'll want to come to honest terms with yourself. Acknowledge your dark thoughts, and acknowledge the injury they do to your heart.

And then, if at all possible, reach out to someone. Don't endeavor to carry all of your burdens alone. Look for the light, and moment by moment try to be free of the dark.

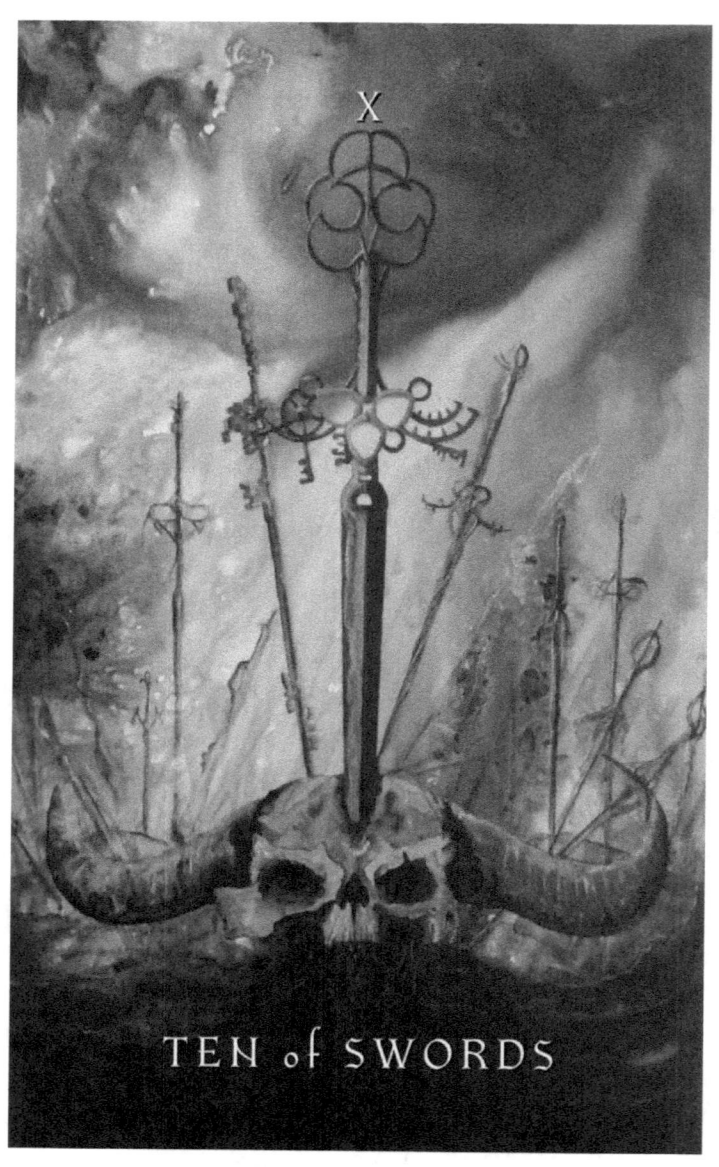

Ten of Swords

The Lowest Point

We reach the point at which we can fall no further.

And the only direction we can climb is up.

The Ten of Swords is that most brutal of cards representing the bottom of all things. Whatever brought you here will likely lead to despair, deep disappointment, and suffering.

These Swords cards...I'm telling you...

You are not alone here. This inevitable place lies in wait for all of us. In life (and in death) there's no avoiding the lows of being human. It will feel tragic. It will *hurt*.

But...

If you really look deeply into the matter, you'll understand that the Ten of Swords is merely an ending, which in all likelihood will soon give birth to a new beginning. You merely need to bridge the gap and survive. Consider this a test of your spiritual durability. Never allow your sense of hope to vanish completely. Until this dark moment has passed, find a light at the end of your tunnel and chase it without giving in.

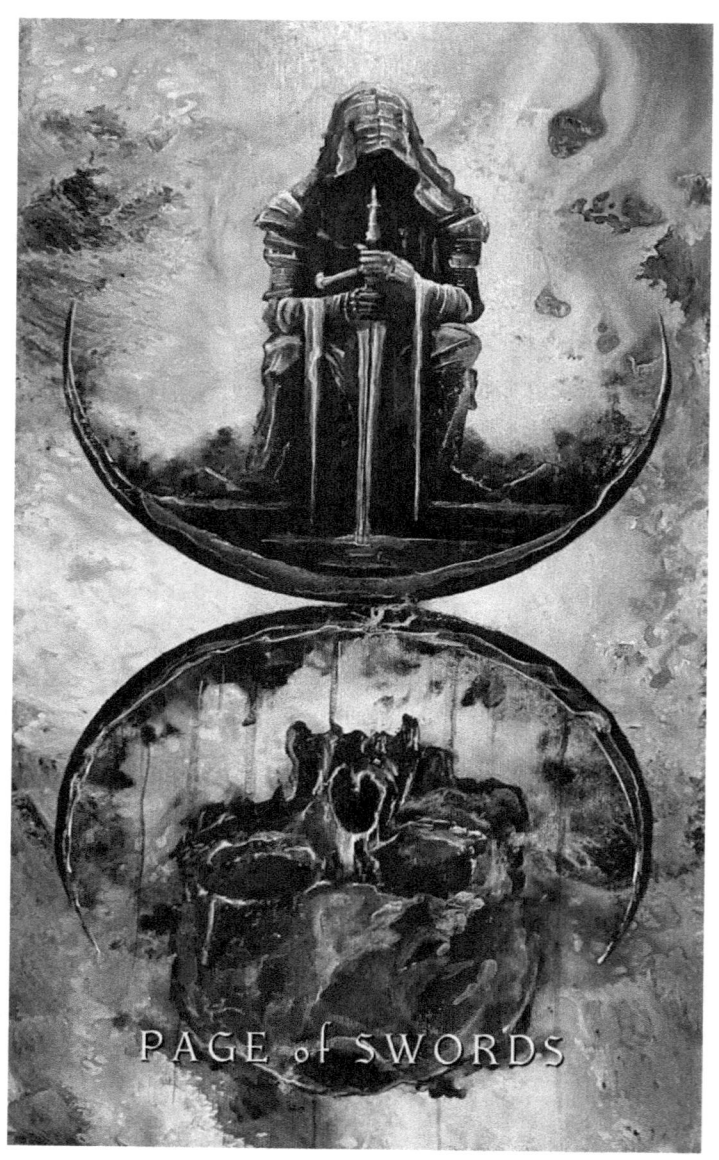

Page of Swords

The Innovator

At last, we've moved beyond all the dark Swords energy.
Now it's time to awaken.
The Page of Swords is all about embracing the power of your mind. The deep waters of your intellect are primed within you, suggesting no better time to:

Learn a new skill.
Hone an existing talent to higher levels.
Enter a new field of study.
Improve and refine the ways in which you work and create.

This is a time to be humble and willing to learn, yet also be somewhat fearless in pursuing your desires. Seek out mentors, invest your creative energy into new projects, and dust any momentary setbacks from your well-armored shoulders.

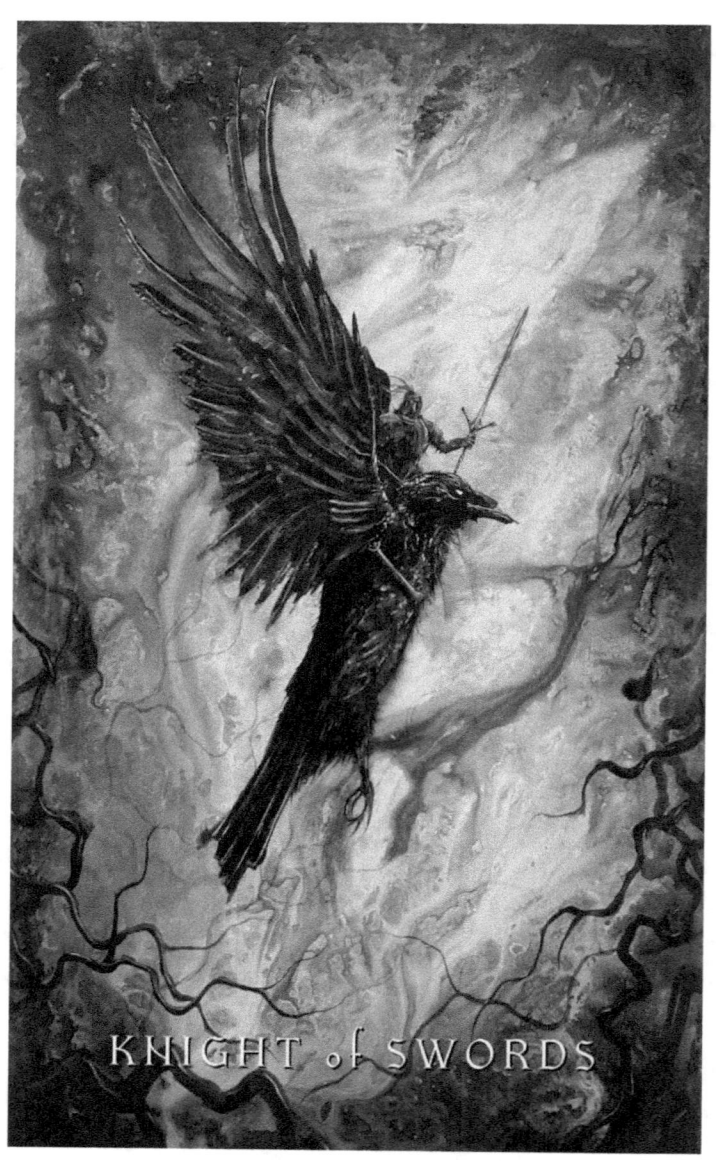

Knight of Swords

Ambition, Raw Power

The suggestion of the Knight of Swords is that, for the moment, you have become *invincible*.

Think of this card as pure, undiluted willpower coupled with swift action. It's no time to sit idly and watch the world sweep past you. Leap on your fastest steed and ride into fray.

You'll be tempted to do these things impulsively, of course. With burgeoning confidence, you may start think of yourself as unbeatable. You'll want to balance this ambition with wise planning. Remain your usual compassionate self, and resist the urge to trample other, well-meaning people on your path to glory.

That said, do NOT go gently into the night. Use this burst of energy to fuel progress in whatever area of life you choose. Set your goals high. Allow your intellect to rise above all else, and see everything as it truly is.

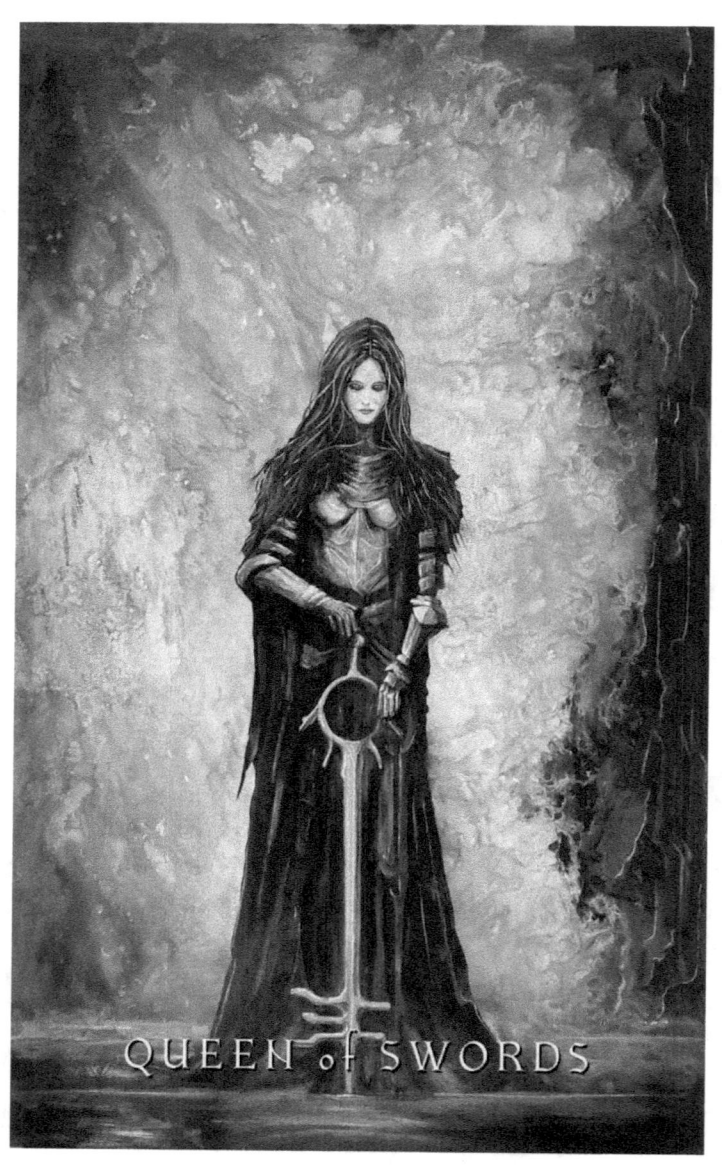

Queen of Swords

The All-Seeing One

The Queen of Swords – master of independence and truth-seeking. To her, the key to success is her ability to consider all the facts and unlock the wisest decision. She listens to intellect rather than to emotions. She desires firm, unbreakable boundaries.

If you pull the Queen of Swords, it's likely you seek some essential truth in your life.

It's time to:
Be direct, even blunt in your communications.
Heed your formidable intellect at all times.
Follow the facts, not your instincts, directly to the truth.

At times, the Queen of Swords may appear cold-hearted or callous. Such directness may offend, and her independent spirit may intimidate. Remember that some people in your life require a tactful approach. In this moment, your communication skills are at their highest. Use this talent to choose your words wisely. Your purpose is to enlighten and unearth the bottommost truth, not to crush all the hearts surrounding you.

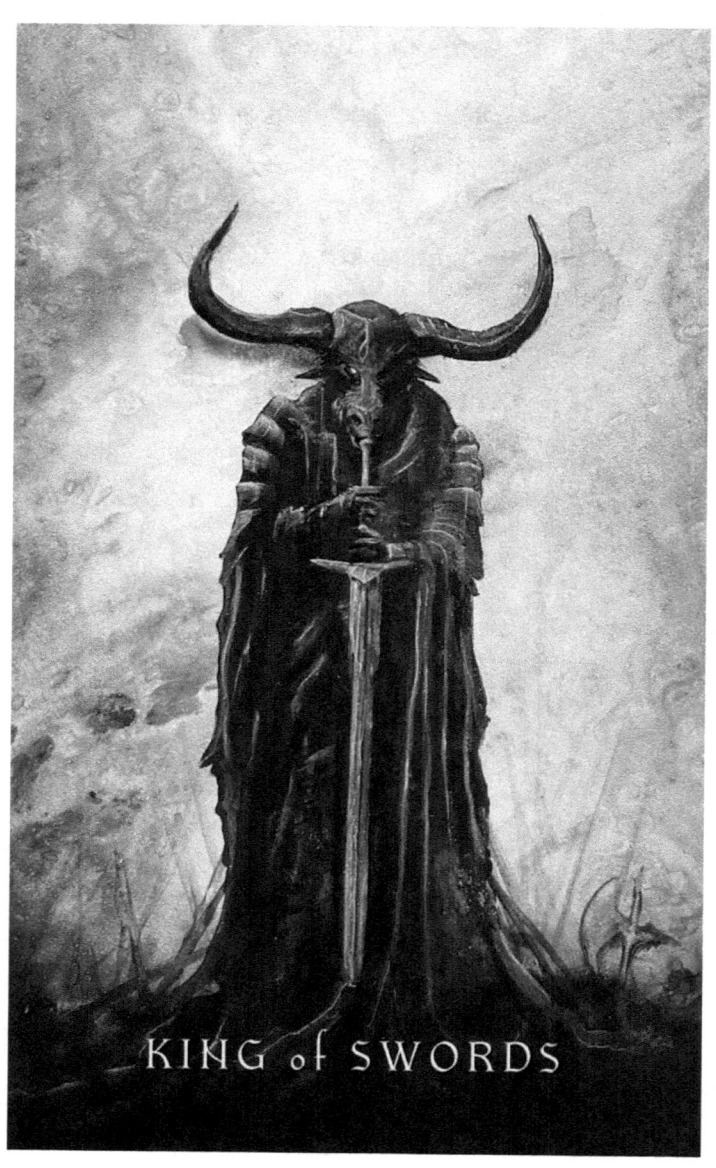

King of Swords

The Thinker

Some leaders are made of charm and charisma, and can sway the masses with a smile.

And yet...

The King of Swords needs no such charm. He's the master of his own mind, holding authority with the twin powers of raw intellect and unparalleled cognizance of all that takes place around him.

When he arrives in your presence, the suggestion is that you have reached the height of your intellectual prowess. You're either in a position of power and respect, or you soon will be. In this moment, others will want to hear what you have to say, and if you speak with conviction and rationality, they will follow.

Of course, absolute power corrupts absolutely. In this moment of formidable intellectual esteem, you'll want to be mindful of your own ego. No one likes a narcissist or a manipulator, even if they're smarter than everyone else in the room. Temper your wits with wisdom. Lead not from the isolation of a mountaintop, but rather side-by-side with those you mean to guide.

Pentacles

The suit of Pentacles focuses on all things of the material world. Your career, your money, your possessions—all buried in the element of earth. You'll need these resources to survive in the world, but you also must learn when to spend...and when to save. Pentacles are pragmatic yet changing in value. The cycle of abundance and scarcity is everlasting.

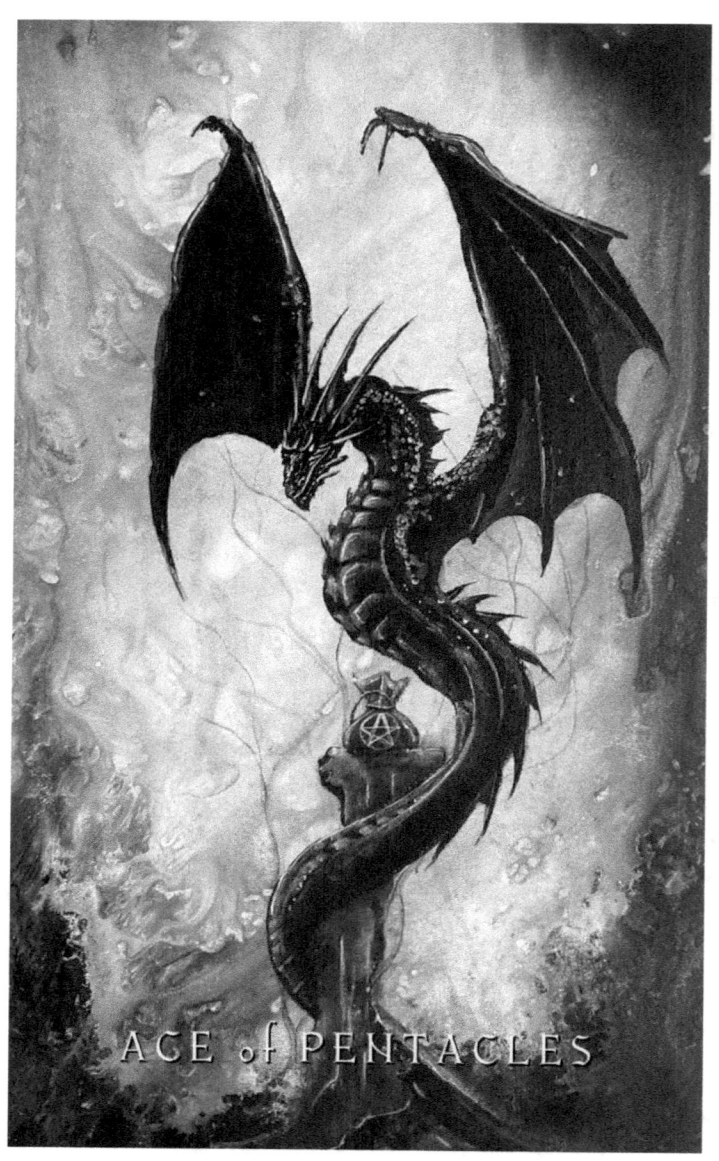

Ace of Pentacles

Hot Prospect

Now we've come to Pentacles. Prepare your pocketbook – we're going to start talking about money. A *lot* of money.

Like all the Ace cards, the Ace of Pentacles implies a new idea or an opportunity to be seized. This time, there's no spiritual or emotional component, but rather a chance to race ahead in strictly physical/material ways.

It portends the chances for:

A new career.
A window of financial opportunity.
A financial windfall.
A positive physical change to your body or life situation.

And, like the other Ace cards, the prevailing wisdom advises that you start crafting a plan. None of the rewards above will come free of charge. They must be earned, ideally through grit and determination. To achieve what you desire, start strategizing immediately.

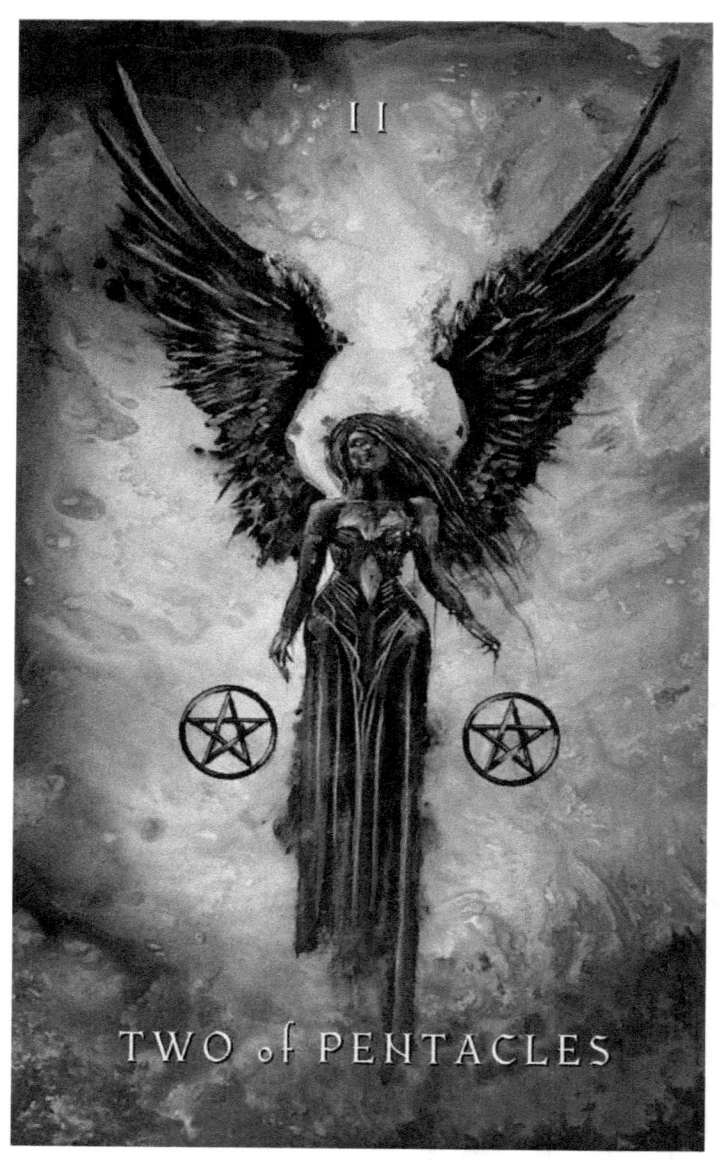

Two of Pentacles

Equilibrium

Slow down, my friend.
Something within you is out of balance.

There is a tendency within highly productive people to always seek greater efficiency, to do more with less, to take on more and more work.
...to do as much as humanly possible.

But we are mortal, and therefore have limits. We are not meant to break ourselves beneath the burden of endless tasks. Too much work and too many people roaming within our orbits causes collisions and conflict.

The Two of Pentacles has a simplistic view of happiness –
Balance in all things. A few strong priorities over a huge variety of obligations. In short, an equilibrium between what you *must* do...and what brings you actual peace and joy.

You have big plans, of course. That's all well and good. But it's high time you make a mental list of all that you do, and decide what needs to stay...and what you can leave in the dust.

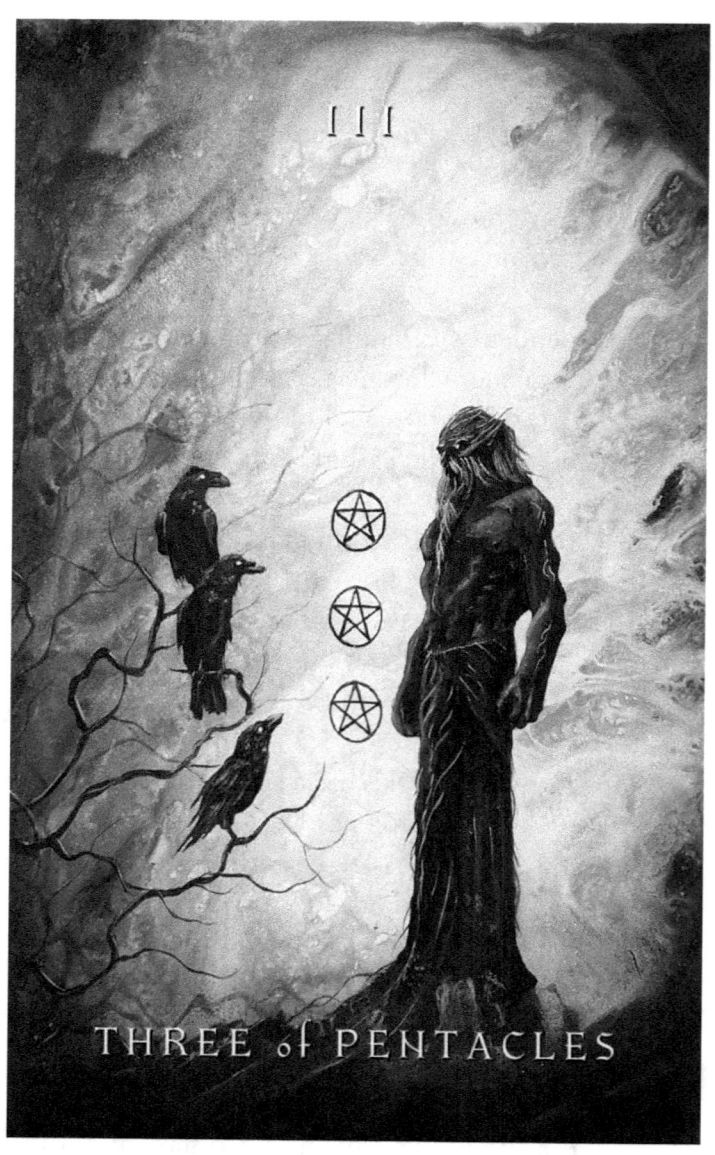

Three of Pentacles

Collaboration

If only we all had a trio of magical ravens representing Wisdom, Courage, and Power to guide us.

Alas, we only have each other.

If ever in your life you were willing to ask for help in achieving a goal, now is the time. Even for those who are fiercely independent, benefits exist to bringing in friends (or even outsiders) to add to the collective experience that is the road to success.

Surely, you *could* go at it alone. But the suggestion of the Three of Pentacles is that your individual skill won't be enough this time. A policy of isolation will slow you down. Diversification, however, will allow you accumulate the abilities of others to your benefit.

The idea is not to be selfish, of course. By adding your talents to those of others, together you have the chance to achieve something greater than any one of you could have done on your own. By themselves, the architect, the stonecutter, and the mortar-maker are but lone craftsmen, but together they can build vast fortresses to stand the test of time.

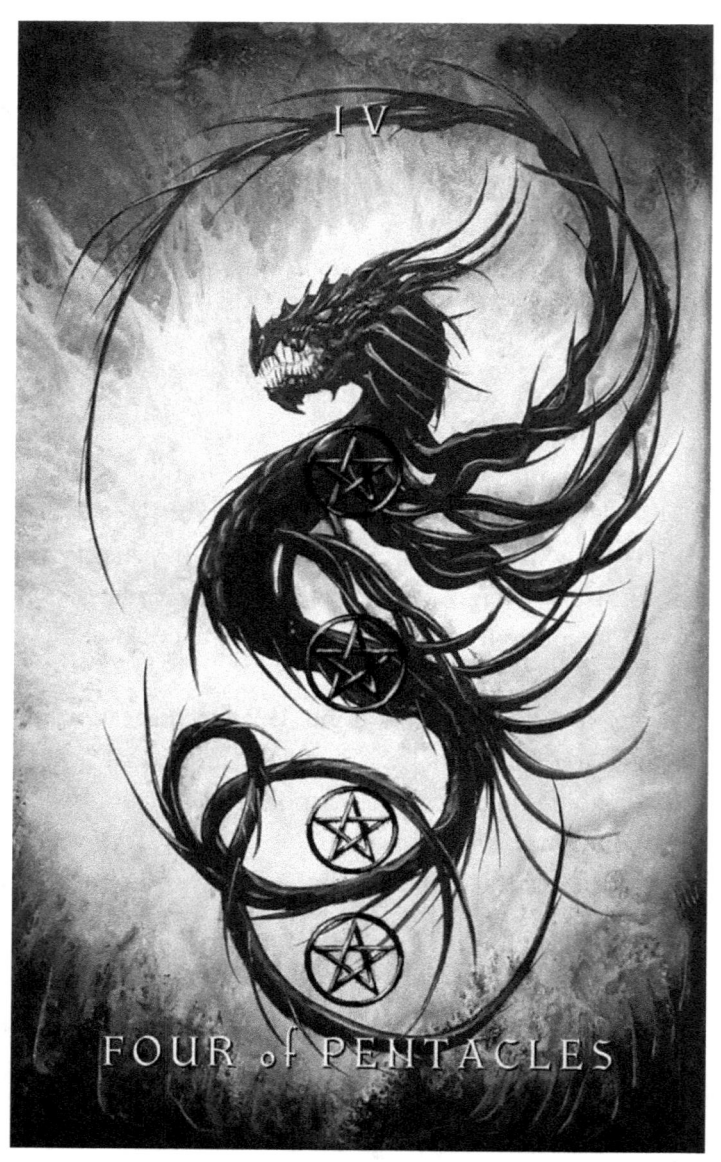

Four of Pentacles

The Control Hoarder

The Four of Pentacles feels like a warning.
It says, '*Hey you. You're spending ALL of your time thinking about money. You're obsessing.*'
Meanwhile, the question you need to ask yourself is –
'*Is this true?*'

On the surface, there's absolutely nothing wrong with wanting to feel secure, with being frugal, with gathering and conserving resources.

However...

The Four of Pentacles suggests you've taken it a little too far. The implication is not merely that you're worried about money, but that you've become controlling in one or more areas of your life. This can extend to your bank account, your family members, and even your romantic partners. You seek safety and security via control, but this isn't a strategy for success. It will inevitably devour you and drive others away.

Remember this: fear of losing something doesn't result in that something being more secure.

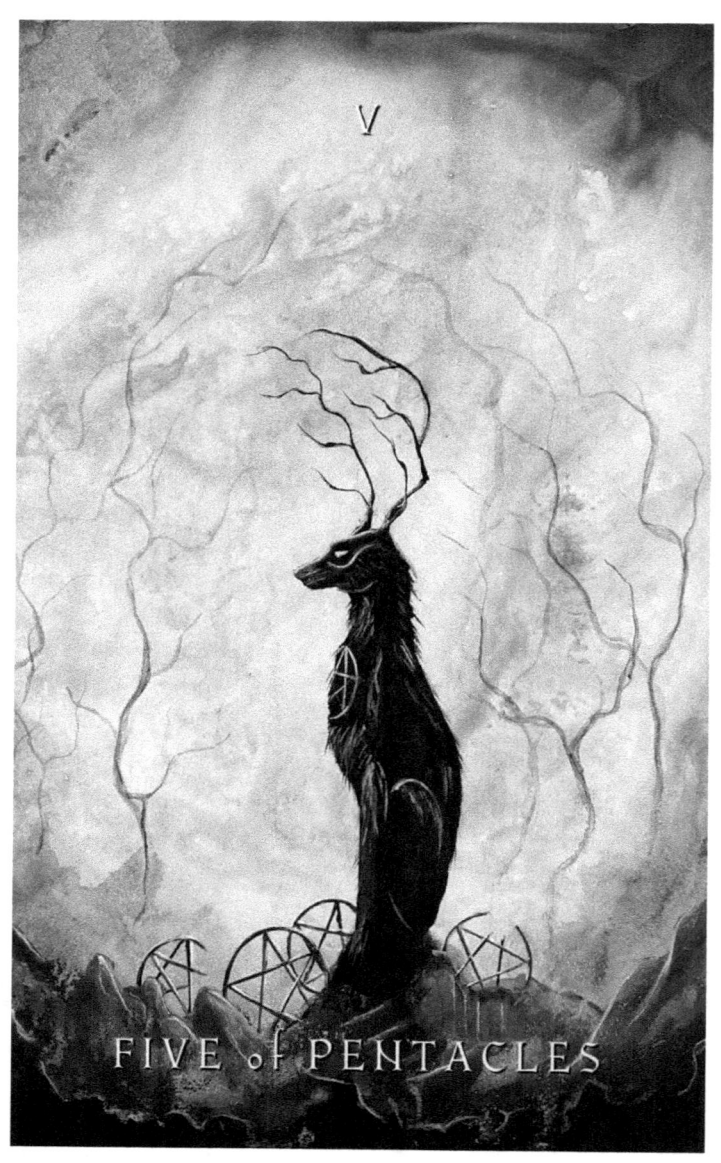

Five of Pentacles

The Cost of Being Alive

Even the strongest among us suffer loss. The transient nature of our existence guarantees that at some point (or more likely several points) in our lives, the things we love will leave us. The Five of Pentacles recognizes this and seeks to prepare us. In being human, you might assume bad luck, but the truth is – to live is to lose. Ill fortunes are just as natural as lucky streaks.

Some of the things you may lose:

A beloved friend or family member
A cherished lover
Your health
Your financial security
Material possessions

Really, the list of possibilities is too long to acknowledge on paper. In these moments, you'll be tempted to fall into desolation. You might even believe that your ill fortune, which feels like evil, has targeted you and you alone. But it's not true. Even the darkest of nights must always end. The sun will rise again, and the sooner you remember it, the better.

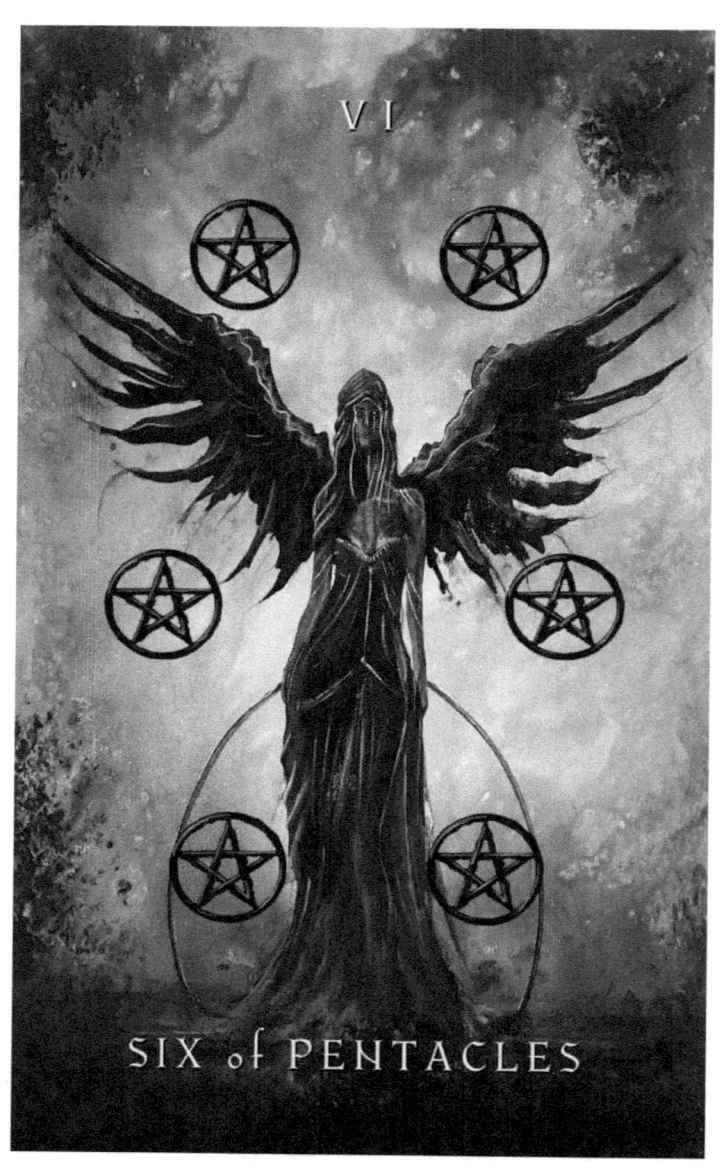

Six of Pentacles

Charity

The Six of Pentacles, angelic and equitable, suggests two meanings. It may mean that, having rebounded from the tragic Five of Pentacles, you find yourself in a place where you're able to help others. This may be financial, or it may be that you are able to offer your time and energy. Your experience with personal loss will qualify you to understand and give aid to those who suffer likewise.

Alternately, the Six of Pentacles may appear when you are able to benefit from someone else's generosity. You've pushed through the shadows of the Five of Pentacles, and now you need help getting back on your feet. If it comes to you, receive it with grace.

If you're the giver, consider offering your help unconditionally. This is no time to seek reciprocation. The authentic soul seeks not to have a transactional relationship with their fellow humans.

If you are the recipient of help from others, do not linger long in a state of needing support. Seek to rise from the ashes stronger than before, and pay it forward to those in need.

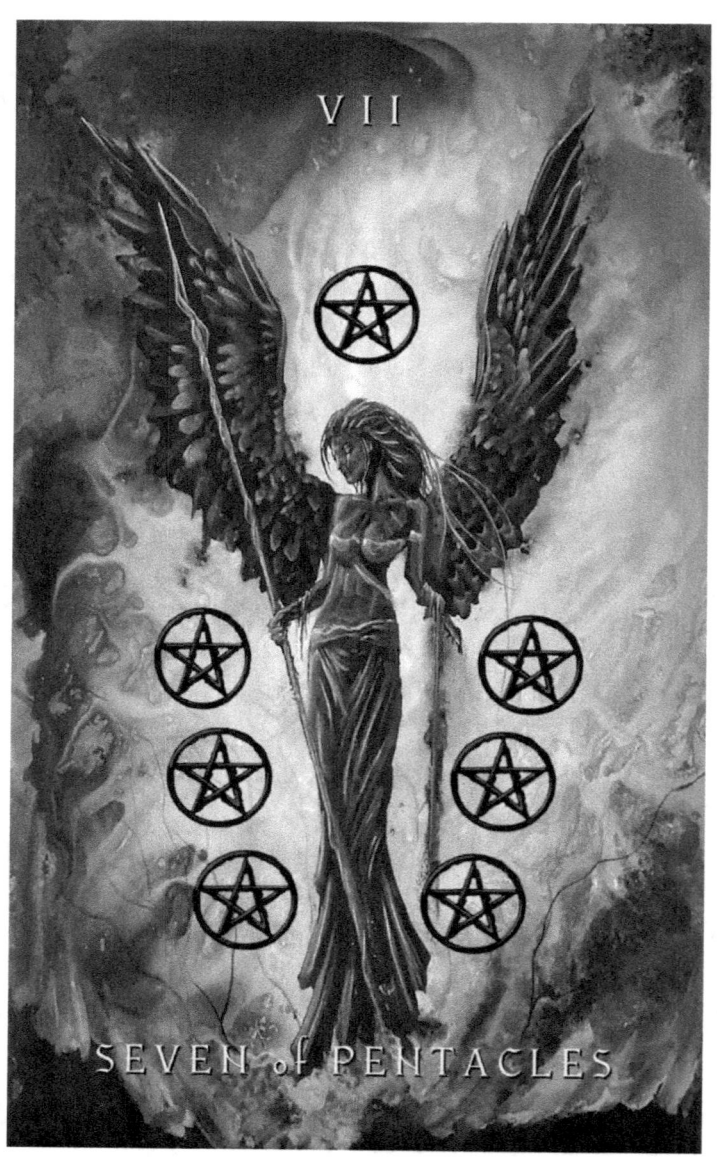

Seven of Pentacles

Slow & Steady Wins the Race

The best things in life are worth waiting for, right?

Personally, I would amend this to say, 'The best things in life are worth *working* for.'

There are those of us who toil for today, who desire immediate results. And then there is the Seven of Pentacles, who prefers a well-structured plan of action to serve both today *and* tomorrow.

It may be that you're already standing on the precipice of an achievement. A few steps higher, and you'll reach the pinnacle. Or it may be true that you've quite a lot of work remaining to reach the top. Weeks, maybe, or even months. No matter. With the Seven of Pentacles fluttering at your side, be assured that as long as you continue putting forth your best effort, your toils will likely culminate in success.

Of course, there are no guarantees. Your greatest assets in these moments? Patience coupled with endurance. Allow yourself to celebrate the small milestones, but all the while keep your eyes centered on finishing whatever it is you desire to do.

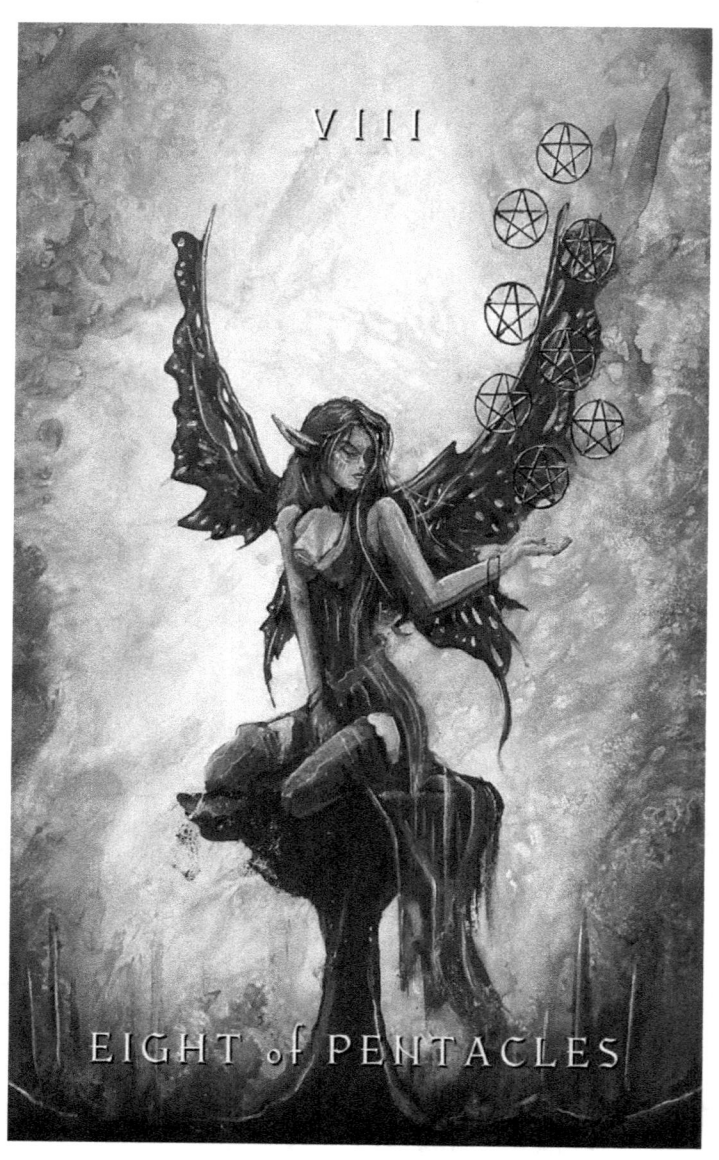

Eight of Pentacles

The Student Becomes the Master

At some point in life, we must all make a choice:

To be somewhat skilled at a variety of different things.

Or...

To become master of one singular endeavor.

The dream of the Eight of Pentacles is that you set aside your small, half-hearted devotion to all the little things you do...

...and seek perfection in one chosen craft.

Naturally, you'll want to remember the lesson of the Two of Pentacles, which urges a balance between work and life. To achieve this, it's likely you'll need to clip the wings off of your lesser activities. If you're not truly devoted to something, now is the time to brush it aside. With these distractions removed, you'll have the ability to focus on your truest passion, whatever it may be.

And, since we're in the heart of the Pentacles suit, you might be happy to discover that if your chosen field of mastery is related to a profession, a creative pursuit, or a particular skill, you'll likely stand to gain financially once you reach the top of your field.

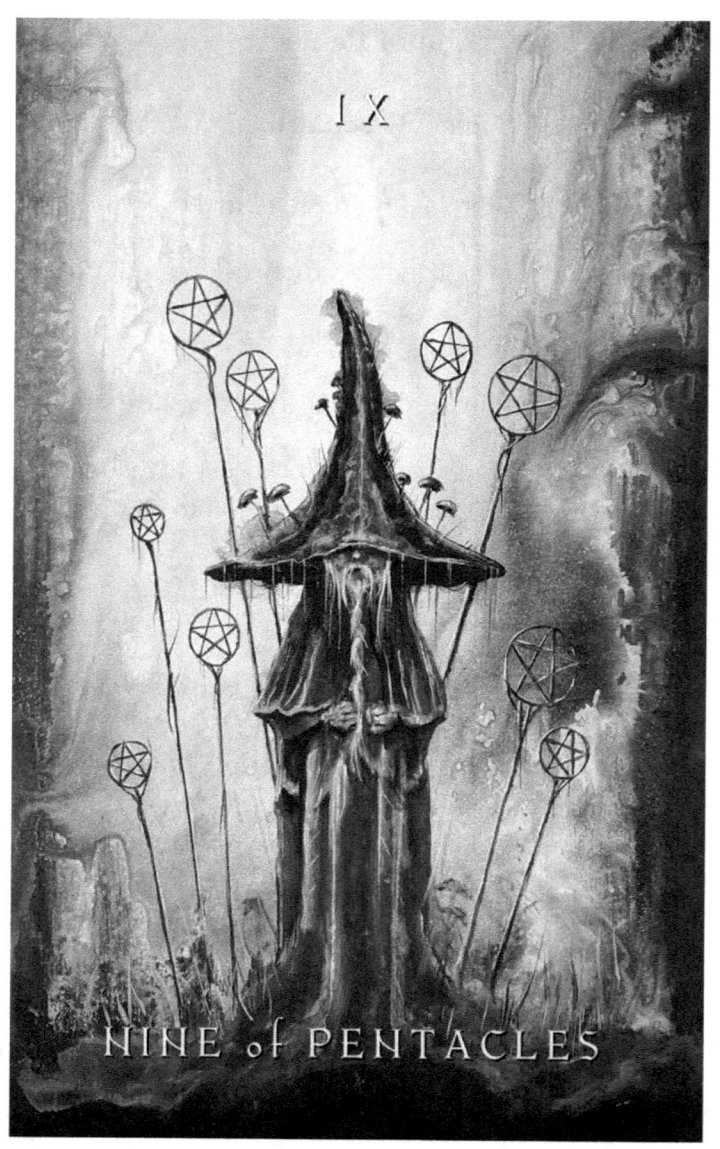

Nine of Pentacles

At Last, Abundance

The hope is, when you encounter the Nine of Pentacles, you're ready for a breather.

The Nine of Pentacles recognizes your life's hard labor, and reveals that at last you're free to enjoy the fruits of your industrious determination. Through effort and focus of will, you've earned success and created the groundwork of wealth and comfort.

Now could be the time to reap the rewards of all your work. Such moments of relaxation are uncommon, and to be utterly enjoyed.

Perhaps it's not financial wealth which has found you, but instead harmony with some aspect of the world surrounding you. This too can be savored, if only for a while. No reward is better than peace of mind, after all, especially when it's hard-earned.

When it comes to an end, and if you find you must return to your toils, never forget what you've learned here. You've laid the bricks of a solid foundation. Build atop these, climbing ever higher, so that the next time the Nine of Pentacles calls upon you, your reward will be even larger.

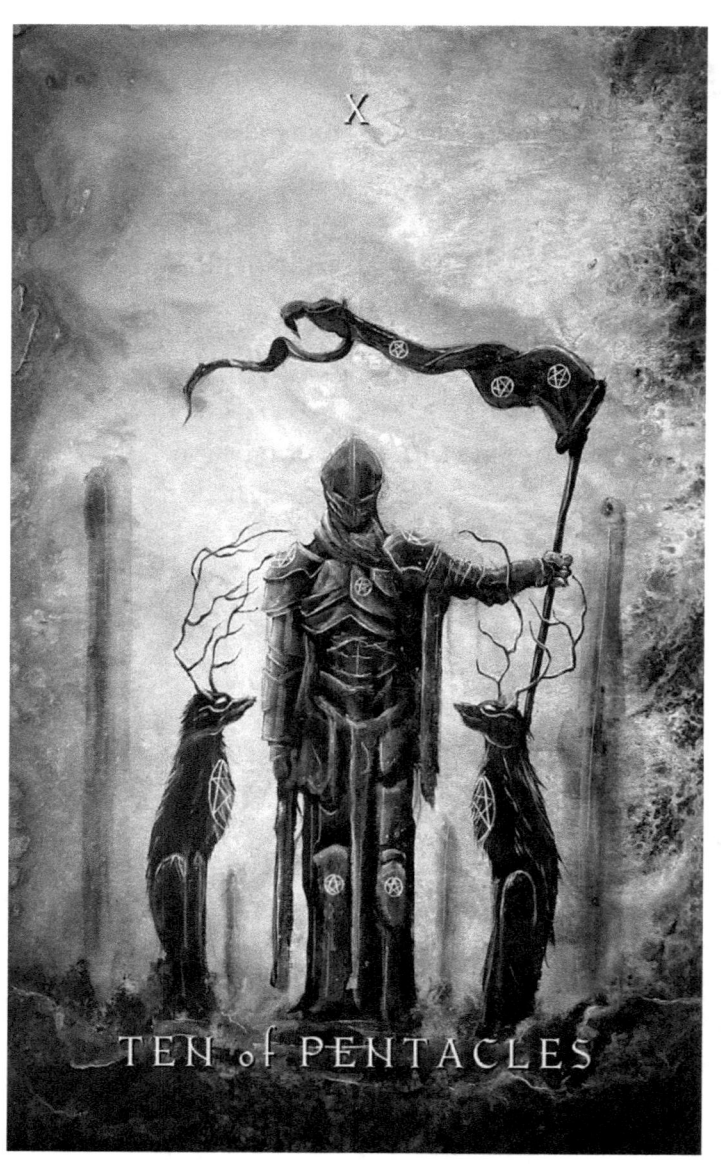

Ten of Pentacles

Completion

In case you haven't noticed, you've done something (or you're *about* to do something) which will have permanence in the world. This is your legacy moment. You're going to make your mark, so to speak.

The most fortunate and skilled among us use their lives to touch the world around them in a way that transcends the individual self. The Ten of Pentacles suggests that due to some effort of yours, you've made an impression on other people that may last more than a single generation.

Perhaps...

You've built a foundation of wealth or experience strong enough to support many family members.

You've gifted someone with unforgettable memories.

You've achieved something bigger than yourself which will affect people beyond what you can imagine.

Remember that you now possess the power to impact people around you. Strive to make this impact a positive one. Do not linger in pride. Rather, sustain the same effort which brought you to this place, and know that the world will be better for it.

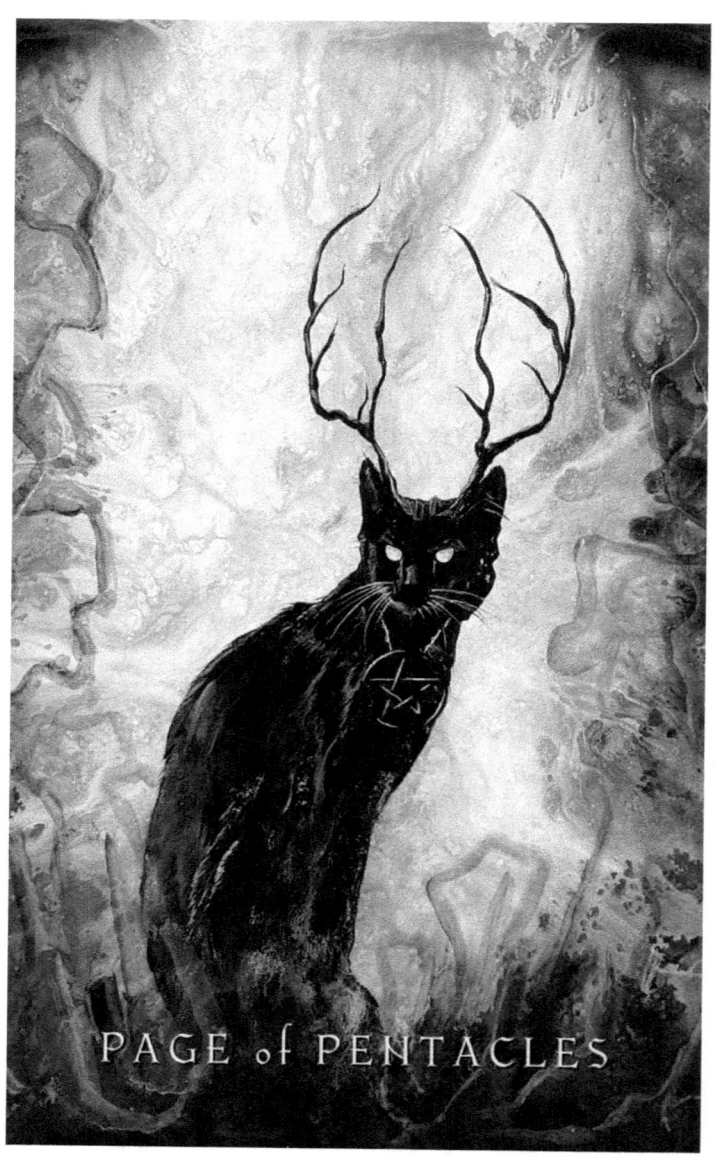

Page of Pentacles

Motivation

Ah, young Page. So fresh and full of life.

The Page of Pentacles suggests, like all its cousin pages, a new beginning. Poking, prodding its way into the world, it searches for material gain, abundant health, and its place firmly secured in the world.

The Page of Pentacles is new here, but is not to be underestimated. If you've pulled this card at the right time and place, you're primed for a new awareness in the ways of manifestation.

Meaning, you're ready not merely to dream, but to *do*.

These are earliest steps of a new journey. The kitten may be clumsy, but it's bold, and soon enough with furious effort it will become a *cat*. This is you, perhaps inspired to start a new journey and create a new self-image. Perhaps you're weary of middling around at the feet of others, and you're ready to grow stronger.

Just remember – nothing is promised. The goals you seek to manifest will only be as marvelous as you strive to make them.

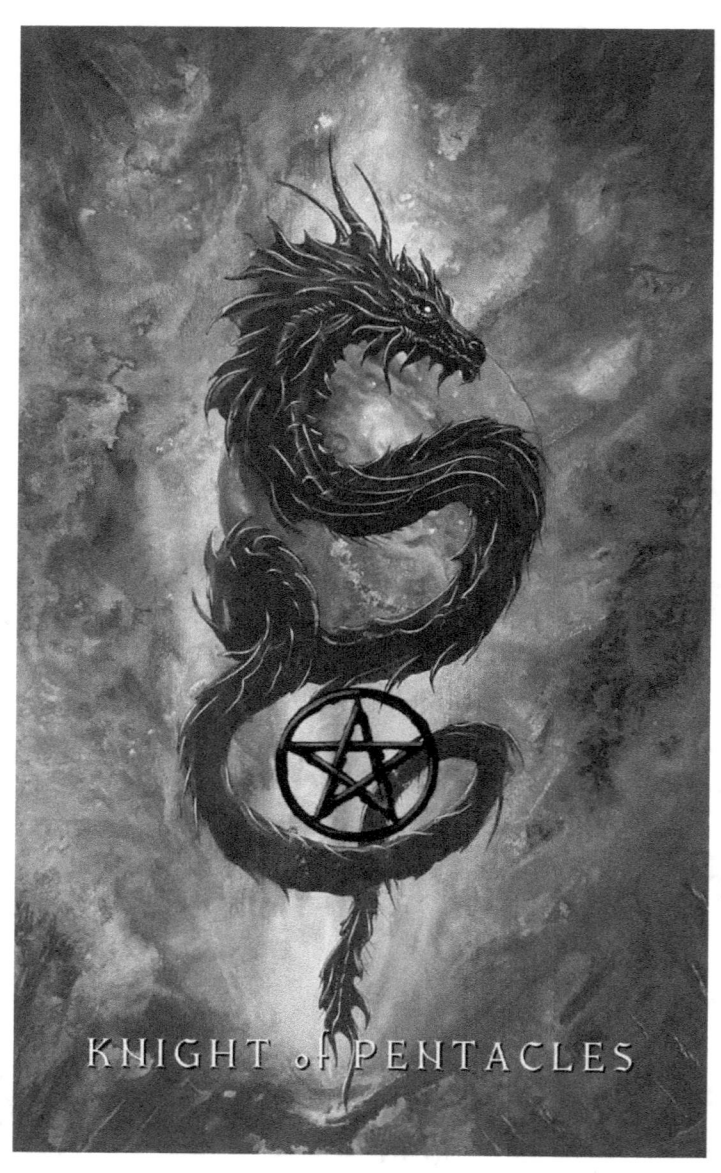

Knight of Pentacles

Responsibility

Perhaps you've been led to believe that Pentacles are dull, money-obsessed, and overly concerned with the mind rather than the heart. It may seem especially true of the Knight of Pentacles, with his tendency to stay the course no matter which direction external forces desire him to move.

The Knight of Pentacles is powerfully immovable.

Perhaps it represents *you*.

The suggestion here and now is that it's *not* time for great change. On the contrary, what you're doing is working quite well (whether you acknowledge it or not) and there's little need to soar in a different direction.

Relentless, they may call you. Methodical. Routine. Boring.

You'll know when it's time for change. At the moment, even if the grind begins to wear down your patience, the Knight of Pentacles suggests staying the course. Fly straight as an arrow – reach your destination sooner.

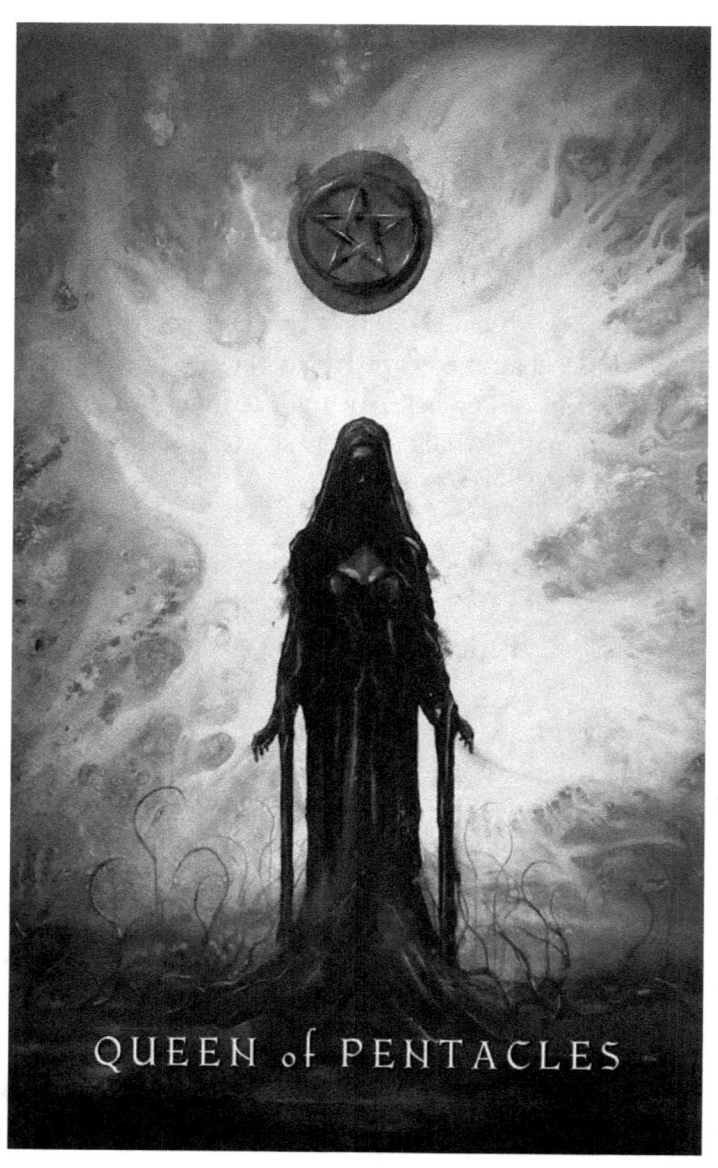

Queen of Pentacles

The All-Mother

Think of all the traits which define a mother:

*Nurturing. Hard-working. Selfless.
Giving. Harmonious. Protective.*

The Queen of Pentacles is somewhat of a paradox. At times, she appears to serve without thought for herself. Her wisdom and generous nature bring comfort to others, and her sense of all things lend her the skill to create peace and balance with ease. And yet, in a way, she's fiercely independent. She's greatly concerned with the welfare of others, yet somehow able to retain her sense of self.

Look closely, and it might be you see some of yourself in the Queen. If not a literal parent, you may find yourself assuming the role of a mother, providing soft landings for children and adults alike. Whole households can be reshaped in your presence, and lives made more secure in the warm light of your nurturing wisdom.

Sound at all like you? If so, assume your role with honor and care. Those you nurture look up to you, and may someday become Queens of Pentacles themselves.

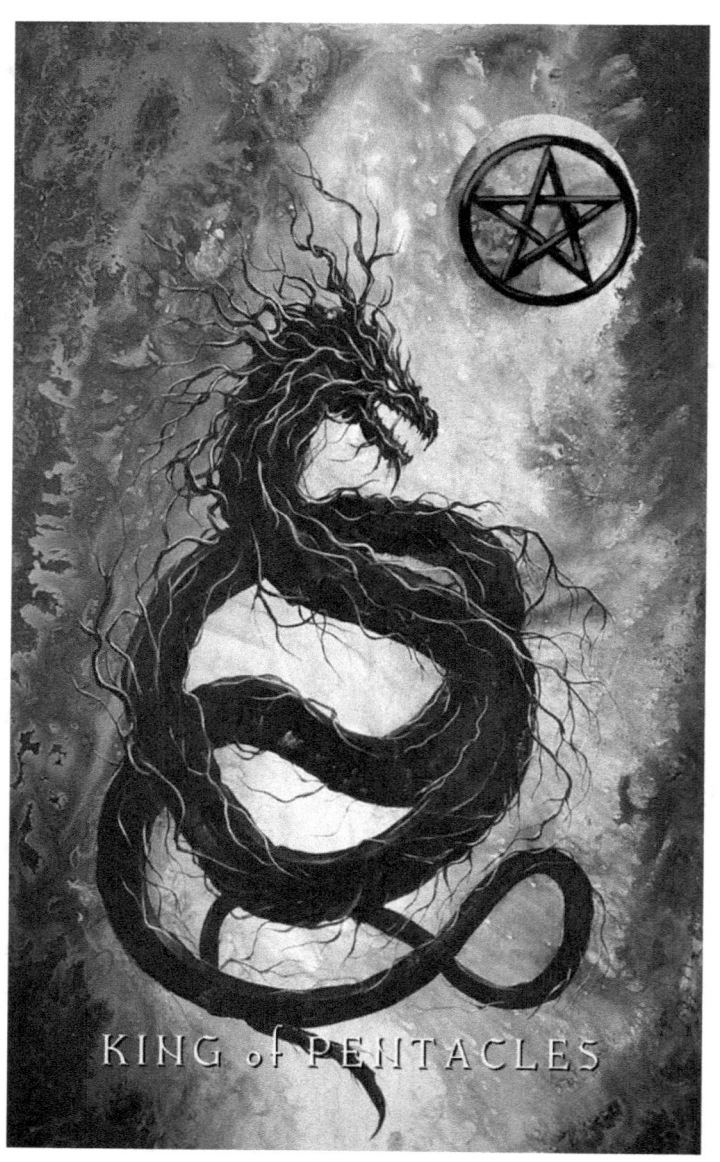

King of Pentacles

The Patriarch

These days, the word 'patriarch' leaves many with a bad taste in their mouths. They see the masculine King of Pentacles energy as brutal, indifferent, perhaps even toxic.

Fortunately, that's not the kind of patriarch I'm talking about.

The energy we should seek is that of a fatherly provider. Certainly, our King of Pentacles is capable of manifesting wealth and material things, but he honors this power by using it to shelter those he loves. His wisdom and ability to navigate the financial world is meant to not to pursue money for money's sake, but to use the power it grants as a boon to his family.

If, in this moment, your energy is that of powerful protector, financial guru, and wise investor in *people*, perhaps you are the King of Pentacles. It's a vast responsibility filling such a role. To toil so hard while evading the trappings of greed and obsession is no easy thing. Remember why you do it. Wealth isn't meant for hoarding. Its truest purposes are the security and freedom it can bring.

Other Decks by J Edward Neill

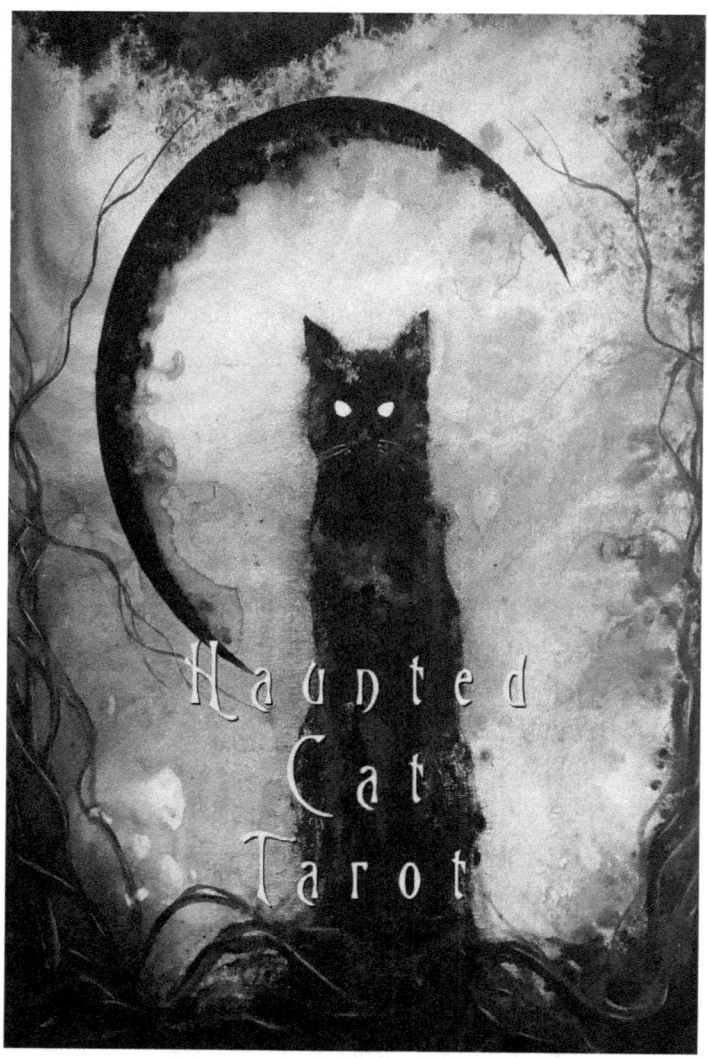

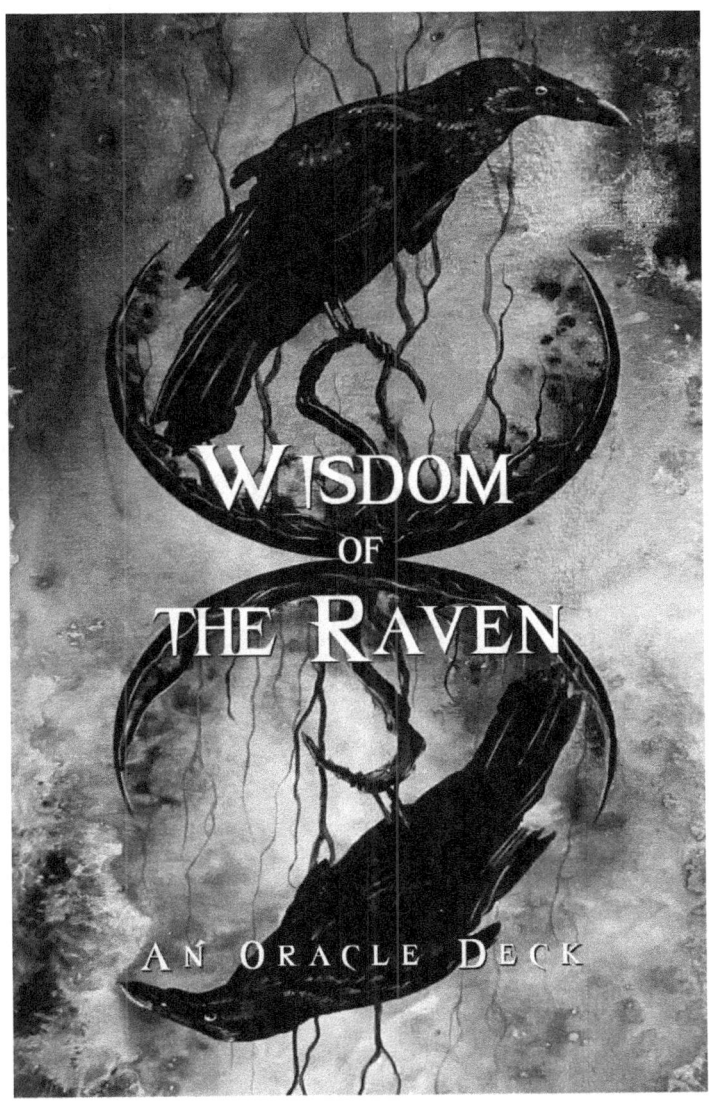

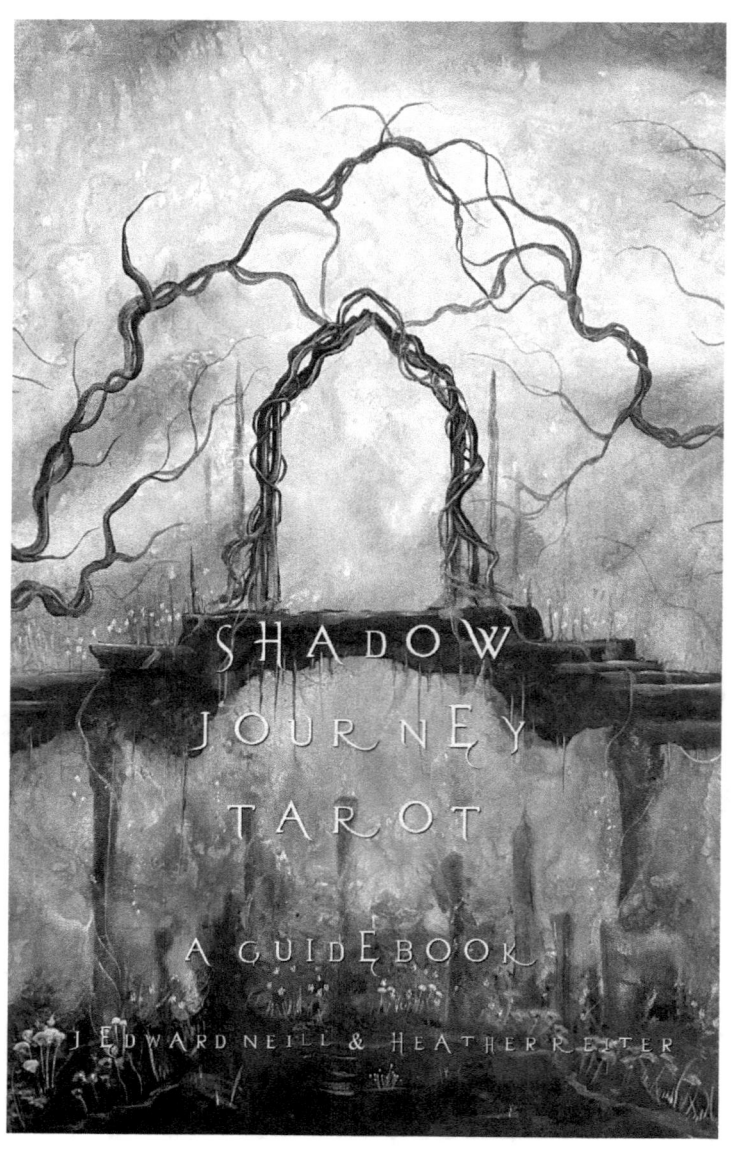

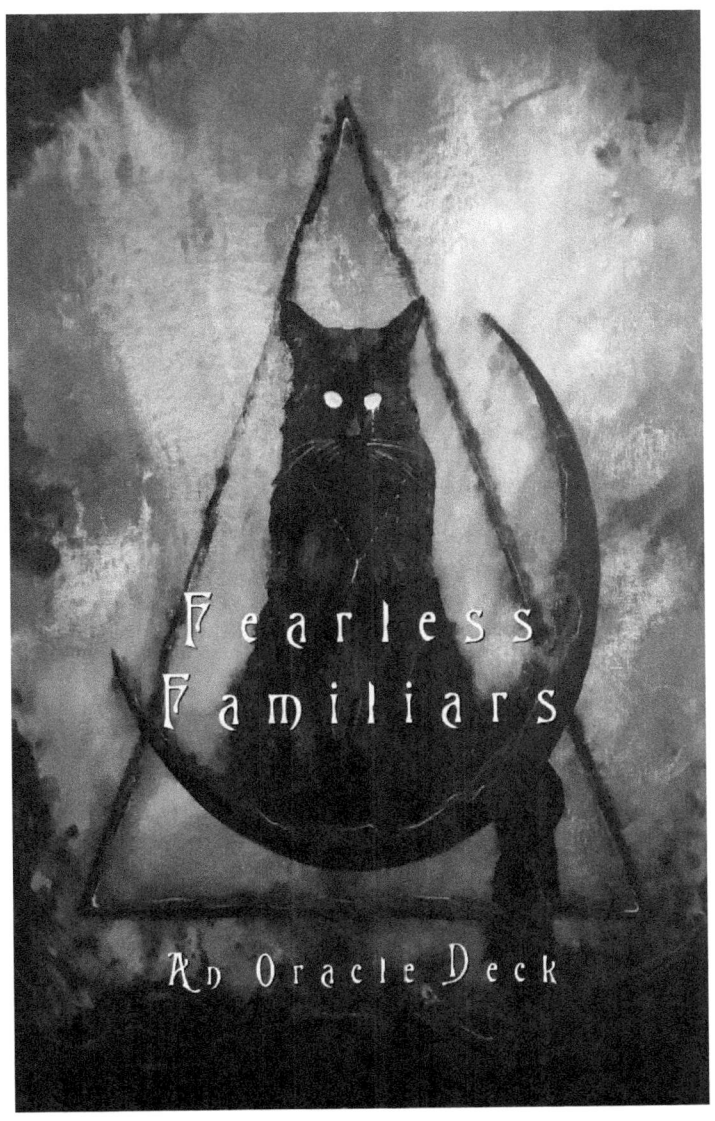

Books by J Edward Neill

The Fall of Castle Carrick
Lords of the Black Sands
A Door Never Dreamed Of
The Hecatomb
Hollow Empire – Night of Knives
Tyrants of the Dead

Card Decks

Spirits & Shadows Oracle
Dreams & Incarnations Oracle
Haunted Cat Tarot
Fearless Familiars Oracle
Wisdom of the Raven Oracle
Shadow Journey Tarot

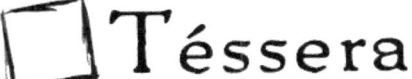 Téssera

www.ingramcontent.com/pod-product-compliance
Lightning Source LLC
Chambersburg PA
CBHW052159220526
45471CB00004B/1739